Creative Approaches to Social Work Practice and Risk

This book bridges together theory and practice to provide practitioners with a creative toolkit to navigate practice, risk, safety and supervision in day-to-day situations.

Each chapter is written by a qualified practitioner, social work academic or someone involved in social work education and presents an innovative or creative approach to risk in social work practice and supervision. Contemporary and diverse ideas, including supervision and ways to work alongside people with lived experience, are explored in a straightforward and innovative way and allow for reflective and insightful practice to take place.

An ideal resource for practitioners looking for quick, innovative, straightforward tools to use in their day-to-day practice.

Heidi Dix is Visiting Senior Research Fellow at the University of Suffolk and Director of the Youth Justice Institute with research interests in youth justice and practice learning.

Aisha Howells is Lecturer and Social Worker with research interests of mothers, child sexual abuse, practice education and creativity in social work.

'Working with risk can be difficult and anxiety-provoking for social work students and practitioners and whilst acknowledging this, this highly recommended practice-based book unpicks some of the key issues that can inhibit or distort professional decision-making involving risk. It is packed with useful information and creative exercises to enhance practitioner self-awareness through self-reflection, team support and supervision, and promote open and effective working relationships inter-professionally and collaboratively with people who use services, to inspire, build confidence and identify positive risk-taking strategies.'

Dr Sue Hollinrake, *Associate Professor, University of Suffolk*

Creative Approaches to Social Work Practice and Risk

EDITED BY HEIDI DIX AND
AISHA HOWELLS

Routledge
Taylor & Francis Group

LONDON AND NEW YORK

Designed cover image: Lauren Carr

First published 2026
by Routledge
4 Park Square, Milton Park, Abingdon, Oxon OX14 4RN

and by Routledge
605 Third Avenue, New York, NY 10158

Routledge is an imprint of the Taylor & Francis Group, an informa business

British Library Cataloguing-in-Publication Data
A catalogue record for this book is available from the British Library

ISBN: 978-1-041-05473-3 (hbk)
ISBN: 978-1-916-92596-0 (pbk)
ISBN: 978-1-041-05474-0 (ebk)

DOI: 10.4324/9781041054740

Typeset in Vectora LT Std
by KnowledgeWorks Global Ltd.

Access the Support Material: www.routledge.com/9781916925960

Contents

Acknowledgements

Our deepest gratitude to Lauren Carr, for creating wonderful illustrations and bringing our ideas to life. You have brought vibrancy to our words, transforming them into unforgettable beauty. We could not have done this without you!

We would like to express our heartfelt thanks to the contributors of this volume. From practitioners, social work academics and those involved in social work education, your creativity and innovation are inspirational. Your fresh ideas have created an immensely useful, practical and evidence-informed book of which we are all proud.

Finally, we would like to dedicate this book to all the Social Workers out there. This book is a tribute to your creativity and courage in a world of practice full of uncertainty and risk. We hope this book sparks your imagination and allows your creative energies to flourish.

Editors

Heidi Dix has been a qualified Social Worker since 1997, has experience of both adult and Children's Services and has worked in both statutory and third sector provision. Heidi was a Senior Lecturer in social work at the University of Suffolk (part-time) for over ten years before leaving in 2022 to take up the position of Director of the Youth Justice Institute. Alongside this she is employed within a youth justice service where she leads quality assurance and workforce development. Heidi is a member of the Youth Justice Board Academic Liaison Network Steering Group. Her interests and publications include social work practice learning and relational practice.

Aisha Howells is a lecturer at the University of Essex and has worked in social work education since 2017. A registered Social Worker, Aisha has previously served as the course lead in social work at the University of Suffolk. Her research interests focus on mothers, child sexual abuse (CSA), domestic abuse, practice education and the use of creative methods in social work. Aisha is passionate about integrating practical insights with innovative approaches to develop high-quality, evidence-informed social work.

Contributors

Shorolla Allen is Assistant Operations Manager within a leadership team in a Youth Justice Service, where her work focuses on effective practice, co-production and addressing disproportionality. As a registered Social Worker since 2020, Shorolla has experience in child protection, kinship care, private fostering, unaccompanied asylum-seeking children and education settings. Shorolla's other areas of focus include training and development, service improvement and developing and utilising innovative and creative methods to achieve sustainable change.

Lauren Carr leads an Art, Design and Technology Facility in a secondary school in Suffolk. Lauren has written articles for NSEAD's *AD* magazine and for the *International Journal of Art Education*. She has been involved in the National Society for Art Educations drawing initiative 'Thinking, Expression, Action' and, through this, became part of a national sketch book circle. Lauren continues to complete commissioned drawing and other drawing projects.

Mark Dimes has 40 years' experience working in the care sector and qualified as a Social orker in 1991 (CQSW). He is currently employed as a Learning and Development Advisor with Suffolk County Council and has worked in various roles across Adults and Children's Services. Mark is also Practice Educator and qualified Professional Coach. He enjoys supporting, mentoring and coaching staff and currently commissions, co-ordinates and facilitates learning and development centred in solution-focused approaches.

Rosslyn Dray is Senior Lecturer at Bournemouth University. She has worked there since 2017. Her interests are in supporting students in their practice learning and this aligns with her research exploring the experience of making mistakes in social work practice learning. Ros was an Approved Mental Health Professional and is a registered Social Worker with experience of working with adults with mental health conditions.

Nora Duckett is a social work lecturer at the Open University. The main focus of Nora's practice, teaching and research has been on responding to and improving responses to children at risk of abuse and keeping social justice and children's rights at the forefront. Prior to her current post, Nora was social work course lead at the University of Suffolk and a senior lecturer in social work at Anglia Ruskin and London Metropolitan Universities. Nora's practice experience includes developing services and working with children who were being sexually exploited and running away from home. Nora has also carried out research and evaluation projects, including a three-year comparative study into youth homelessness in four European countries, and co-authored two editions of 'Proactive Child Protection and Social Work' (2008/2016 Sage).

Nicola Print is a qualified Social Worker and Practice Approach Development Manager. She has extensive experience in Children's Services, having worked in frontline social work, with her last position being a team manager. Nicola has presented at two international Signs of Safety gatherings, where she shared her experience of working with people from a strengths-based and relational approach. Her goal is to empower practitioners to excel in their roles, ensuring they have the skills and knowledge needed to make a positive impact in their communities.

Dhriti Sarkar is licenced Clinical Psychologist from India with experience in providing psychotherapeutic, diagnostic and psychoeducational services in community organisations, public healthcare systems and in private practice. She also has experience working in advocacy and public engagement programmes for mental health in India. Her research interests lie in uncovering barriers and catalysts for individuals engaging with mental health services and the application of brief psychotherapy in low-resource settings.

Sophie Walters is an accredited psychotherapist with extensive experience across NHS and private practice settings. Her therapeutic focus includes specialised support for LGBT+ individuals and those navigating complex trauma. Her research interests include the integration of lived experience perspectives in mental health research and social work. Sophie combines evidence-based therapeutic approaches with empathy and practical applications, to enhance outcomes across diverse clinical and community contexts.

A note about illustrations

This book is centred on different and diverse creative approaches, specifically how learning can often be enriched through using visual elements. As such, we have repeated illustrations throughout the chapters indicating specific sections that we believe are important for you as practitioners to know, so that you can use the tools to their maximum potential. Although the names of the headings may be different or within a different order within each chapter, the illustration speaks to the detail below:

	Tool An introduction to the tool. This provides a brief *overview*.
	Inspiration Where the inspiration for the tool is drawn from. This is the tool's *origins*.
	Theory The theoretical perspective which underpins the tool. This is social work practice being *evidence-informed*.
	Example Where an example is provided of the tool being used. This brings the *tool to life*.
	Application The description of putting the tool into practice. This is the *how-to*.

	Other ways to use the tool
	Shows you how to use the tool between a practice educator and learner. This is about *education*.
	3 Key Points
	Outlines three key take away learning points. This is the *summary*.

Figures

Tables

Appendices

The following list of appendices can be accessed and downloaded online at the Routledge book page: www.routledge.com/9781916925960

Introduction

Heidi Dix and Aisha Howells

Working with risk and complexity in social work can be scary and anxiety provoking. The political climate that social work operates within means that if things go wrong, the results can be life changing for everybody involved and this

DOI: 10.4324/9781041054740-1

is often what practitioners and students are most concerned about. However, working with risk can also be stimulating and challenging and is prevalent in most, if not all, areas of social work practice. This book draws on traditional principles of identifying and managing risk through fresh and creative approaches and provides practical exercises and tools to assist practice.

DEFINING RISK

Disciplines such as health, probation, police and social care can hold contrasting views when they refer to risk and often professionals have differing ideas regarding its assessment and management. Risk can also carry differing meanings depending on the practice area of social work. The divergence between organisations and teams often goes unrecognised and/or unacknowledged by practitioners with the result being that intra- and inter-professional working could be affected. An example of a difference in focus can be seen in the practice area of youth justice which sits between both criminal justice and safeguarding systems. Risk assessment in this context considers the safety and wellbeing of the child alongside the safety and wellbeing of actual and potential victims as well as assessing the child's future offending behaviours. However, other disciplines may have a focus on either keeping the child safe (children's social care services), protecting the public (police), or may have an entirely different emphasis altogether. All are talking about identifying harm and safety and therefore a shared understanding of what we mean when we refer to risk is an important place to start. There are many different definitions of risk; however, one that will be used for the purpose of this book is as follows: "The probability that an event or behaviour carrying the possibility of an adverse or negative outcome will occur" (Kemshall, 1998, pv).

RISK AND SOCIAL WORK PRACTICE

Areas where social work is practised can be broadly divided into adult and community care, criminal justice and child protection (Barry, 2007) and in terms of risk they have different histories, preoccupations and approaches as seen in Table 0.1. Whatever the discipline, understanding organisational culture and preoccupations regarding the complexity around risk assessment and risk management is an important part of supervision and providing a safe space to explore this is essential.

Table 0.1 Areas of social work practice, influences and approaches

Area of social work practice	Influences	Approach
Criminal Justice	This is heavily influenced by the media and public concern.	Arguably, this area of practice has the most risk assessment tools. Risk assessments are often actuarial (based on statistics), rather than constructed on clinical judgements, or are a combination of both. A focus has been towards managing and containing risk rather than resolving behavioural issues. However, this is changing through a recognition of the impact of structural inequalities such as poverty and racism and the need to address these as part of the assessment and management of risk.
Adult and Community Services	Influences include people who use services.	Predominant model is one of positive risk taking, rather than risk minimisation with an emphasis on a strengths-based approach. In recent years policies and practice models emphasise the importance of co-production and the right for people to have a voice and control over their lives.
Child Protection	Often influenced by media and public concern following the publicity that follows a child death reported in the media.	It has been criticised in the past as focussing too much on bureaucracy and processes (Munro, 2011). It can also be argued that this area of practice has historically focussed on a narrow view of risk to the child within a family context, although this is changing with an understanding of the risks posed to children and young people outside of the home – and the need to consider extra-familial harm (Firmin, 2017).

Source: Adapted from Effective Approaches to Risk Assessment in Social Work: An International Literature Review (Barry, 2007).

EVIDENCE-INFORMED PRACTICE VS EMPATHY AND INTUITION

Ideas of risk are often based on binary concepts and there is extensive research that helps us to understand risk identification and management. Put simply, this includes the need to be clear about who is at risk, the identification of the risk (what it is), how likely it is to happen (imminence), when it can happen (context), what the impact will be (severity) and what will increase and decrease the risk. Effective risk management often includes having effective safety and contingency plans in place. It can also include external controls being applied to manage the situation whilst internal controls are being developed, e.g. the use of supervised contacts for parents in the child protection arena whilst they are attending parenting courses to develop the knowledge and skills to care for a child and/or participating in recovery services to manage substance misuse.

Linked to the focus on risk assessment and management in modern social work is the suggestion as to how much our emotions can and do inform the professional judgements that we make (Ingram, 2012, 2015; Munro, 2008; Taylor, 2017). A longstanding debate is whether social work practice is informed by evidence and research at one end of the spectrum, often referred to as the 'head', or whether it is informed by empathic and intuitive understanding at the other end, 'the heart', and it can often feel as if never the twain shall meet (Munro, 2008). However, to assess and manage risk effectively, Munro suggests that a combination of the two is required. For example, if a social worker needs to write a formal report to access funding or to assist the Court to decide a course of action, they need to be able to draw upon their logic and knowledge base. However, if to complete the report, a piece of work needs to be undertaken collaboratively with a child or adult, the ability to empathise and 'tune in' to establish an effective relationship to obtain the information required will necessitate the use of our intuitive understanding (Munro, 2008). We of course need to be able to tune in to ourselves as well (Taylor and Devine, 1993) to better understand and manage our emotional responses to identify and manage risk effectively and this book contains a number of tools to assist with this.

KNOWING WHAT WE BRING TO THE ASSESSMENT AND PLANNING PROCESS

To support positive change, as well as understanding ourselves, we also need to recognise what we bring to our work. This includes thinking about our own experiences, beliefs, values and consideration of any cognitive bias. For example, we may bring our own individual lived experiences and therefore need to carefully think about the influence of these within our thinking, interactions and practice. Supervision is one way that is considered necessary to explore these and ensure that everyone is kept safe. Conscious and unconscious bias are usually developed through our experiences, feelings and how we view the world. Assumptions and stereotypes can affect our work and negatively affect the judgements we make. There are several biases which can affect our decisions and some of these are outlined below:

- *Confirmation bias* – this is where we may be unable to see or accept information that counters an original or underlying judgement that we have made about a child and this can lead to self-fulfilling prophecy, e.g. if we have low aspirations for a child, we are more likely to find evidence to fit this view and ignore information that may contradict this.
- *Attribution theory* – the idea that if we relate to, or are similar in some way to a person, e.g. age, gender, ethnicity, we are more likely to locate problems as being external to them and find explanations for their behaviour. However, if people are different from us in some way, we are more likely to locate any problems they have as being internal to them and linked to their personality. For example, we may believe a child is choosing to behave in a certain way, rather than identify they are being criminally exploited.
- *Halo effect* – we become so tuned in to identifying and building strengths, we do not recognise the risks they pose to others. Many people we work with hold dual identities, and as well as being vulnerable may also pose a risk to others.
- *Availability bias* – a tendency to rely on information that is readily and easily accessible without gathering information from a variety of sources.
- *Anchoring effect* – is where we can rely too heavily on or 'anchor' to one trait or piece of information when making decisions, another reason why gathering information from a range of sources is necessary as it can help to counterbalance this.
- *Bandwagon effect* – views expressed by dominant members of the team/ managers/other professionals may influence the judgement of the practitioner rather than evidence.

A BRIEF OVERVIEW OF THE BOOK CONTENTS

This book offers ideas beyond traditional approaches to the identification and management of risk to help practitioners to work in different ways with people to support positive outcomes. The intention of this book is to provide a resource for practitioners to effectively work with the uncertainty that contemporary social work brings and each chapter contains the following:

- Standalone tools to promote individual and group reflection to aid decision making
- A brief description of each tool and how it can be used in different ways and in different settings
- The theoretical frameworks that inform the development of the tool

In Chapter 1, Print helps us to consider our emotional responses to working with uncertainty and suggests that how information is gathered and interpreted depends to a large extent on our lived experiences. Print draws on the principles of solution-focussed practice to provide tools which enable us to reflect on our thoughts and feelings of working in complex situations and help us to work collaboratively with others to improve safety and wellbeing.

Chapter 2 by Howells addresses the sensitive and challenging topic of Child Sexual Abuse. It can be an emotive area of practice involving high levels of risk where practitioners can lack confidence or shy away from engaging with this matter, despite its critical importance. The chapter provides three original tools for practitioners to enhance their knowledge and critical thinking in practice, alongside practical skills when working directly with a child.

Dray, in Chapter 3, suggests that making mistakes is an inevitable part of developing, effective, social work practice. Three innovative tools help us to re-examine our relationship with making mistakes, exploring our thoughts and feelings in our approach to mistakes and the risk in trying something new. There is consideration of the support we need to manage any uncertainty and evaluation of our role, to draw learning and insight from making mistakes.

Within Chapter 4 Duckett outlines professional dangerousness patterns and characteristics that have been identified over time and provides tools to help practitioners to analyse their intuitive feelings to support professional curiosity and challenge stereotypes, assumptions and biases. Duckett argues that well-resourced teams working together to develop multi-agency plans are necessary to effectively provide positive outcomes.

Allen, in Chapter 5, acknowledges that working with uncertainty often means that we need to engage in conversations with others that can challenge us as they seem difficult and feel uncomfortable. These conversations involve people with lived experience, managers, colleagues and practitioners from different disciplines as well as managers. This chapter offers three tools to aid the development of reflective and relational practice to aid effective communication which enables us to hold 'difficult conversations' to assess and address risk.

The value of therapeutic techniques in social work can be significant and Chapter 6 by Walters and Sarkar highlights the centrality of practitioner's relationships with the individuals they work with. The chapter presents three tools, focussed on the individual's narrative, feedback and endings; all of which are underpinned by a sense of curiosity, both about the individual and ourselves.

In Chapter 7, Dimes challenges us to work collaboratively in supervision and alongside people with lived experience using coaching skills and techniques. There is a reframe of risk towards 'safety and wellbeing' to align with a strengths-based approach throughout the chapter. Three tools have been adapted with reflective activities to develop insight of practitioner strengths and goal setting alongside consideration of our non-verbal communication.

Dix, in Chapter 8, argues that a relational approach is necessary to enable effective decision making and outlines the IDEAS framework to help us to think about the different knowledge, skills, attitudes and personal qualities that evidence suggests are necessary to be an effective, relational practitioner. She also outlines how the IDEAS framework can support practitioners to be anti-racist in their practice. The chapter finishes with a helpful checklist which draws on the IDEAS framework to support practice that is *defensible* rather than *defensive*.

Finally, the tools have been provided as appendices online to access these easily and support creativity within practice.

REFERENCES

Barry, M. (2007) *Effective Approaches to Risk Assessment in Social Work: An International Literature Review*. Scottish Executive. Available at: https://www.homestudycredit.com/courses/contentRM/RM-Effective-Approaches-to-Risk-Assessment.pdf Accessed 26/01/25

Firmin, C. (2017) *Contextual Safeguarding An overview of the operational, strategic and conceptual framework*. Available at: https://www.oscb.org.uk/wp-content/uploads/2019/05/Contextual-Safeguarding-Briefing.pdf Accessed 16/02/25

Ingram, R. (2012) 'Emotions, social work practice and supervision: An uneasy alliance?, *Journal of Social Work Practice*, 27(1), pp. 5–19. https://doi.org/10.1080/02650533.2012.745842

Ingram, R. (2015) *Understanding emotions in social work. theory, practice and reflection*. Berkshire: Open University Press/McGraw-Hill Education.

Kemshall, H. (1998) *Risk in probation practice*. Aldershot: Ashgate.

Munro, E. (2008) *Effective child protection*. 2nd edn. London: Sage publications.

Munro, E. (2011) *The Munro Review of Child Protection: Final Report A child-centred system*. ISBN: 9780101806220 Available at: https://assets.publishing.service.gov.uk/media/5a7b455ee5274a34770ea939/Munro-Review.pdf Accessed 16/02/25.

Taylor, B. (2017) *Decision making, assessment and risk in social work*. London: Learning Matters/Sage.

Taylor, B. and Devine, T. (1993) *Assessing needs and planning care in social work*. Hants, Aldershot: Arena Ashgate Publishing Limited.

Chapter 1
Practising confidently in times of uncertainty

Nicola Print

INTRODUCTION

Social workers who are aware of their perspectives and experiences in handling risk are fundamental to effective risk-sensible practice. In children and families social work, The Working Together to Safeguard Children (HM Government, 2023) guidance places an emphasis on partnership working. This coupled with the National Framework (2003) statutory guidance published by the Department of Education sets the direction for practice in children's social care. The guidance underscores the importance of collaboration among agencies, practitioners and organisations involved in child protection and it encourages joint working to ensure better outcomes for children, through providing early, targeted support to families in need, reducing the need for more intensive interventions (MacAlister, 2022).

Effective risk assessment is crucial for social workers to safeguard vulnerable adults. The Care and Support Statutory Guidance emphasises the importance of promoting wellbeing and preventing abuse and neglect through comprehensive risk assessments. Social workers must identify and evaluate potential risks, considering the individual's circumstances and the likelihood and impact of these risks. This process involves gathering detailed information, collaborating with other agencies, and ensuring that the individual's voice is central to the assessment (Department of Health and Social Care, 2024).

Working inter-professionally is not easy to do. McCreadie et al.'s (2008, cited in Dixon, 2023) research identified that professionals' definitions of abuse and neglect were tactically driven by professional self-interest, making managing risk together a challenge. Colleagues from different sectors often question each other's perceptions and judgements relating to children's, families' and adults' situations. However, more recent research shows that professionals from different disciplines can embrace multidisciplinary working (Braye et al., 2014, cited in Dixon, 2023).

DOI: 10.4324/9781041054740-2

WORKING WITH RISK

There are a variety of risk management frameworks and tools to support the assessment and management of risk. Most are based on collecting and analysing information with often little reference to the practitioners' individual characteristics such as role, gender, class, race and knowledge and how these contribute to risk assessment, management and decision-making. On the contrary, how the information is gathered and interpreted is a subjective process and is dependent on the worker's past and present, social and professional lived experience. Considering all these elements helps social workers to refine their risk assessment skills and ensure their practice remains both effective and ethically grounded. This chapter will outline two tools, **Reflective Risk Management** and **Concern and Strengths Matrices** to help practitioners to identify and work effectively with risk.

RUMBLING WITH VULNERABILITY

'Rumbling with vulnerability' is a concept articulated by Brené Brown, a prominent author and researcher recognised for her studies on vulnerability, bravery, empathy and courage. To rumble with vulnerability is to actively embrace our weaknesses instead of evading or dismissing them. From my experience, 'Rumbling with vulnerability' (Brown, 2018) is often frowned upon in the real world of social work. The term 'they're not resilient' is often used to diminish a worker's status and ability to practise social work. This culture contributes to a reluctance from workers to express or share how they are feeling through fear of being seen as weak or incapable. Brown argues that most people experience courage and fear simultaneously and that during those moments when we feel vulnerable and are pulled between our fear and courage, we need shared language, skills and tools to support us through the 'rumble'.

The **Reflective Risk Management** tool (Figure 1.1) which is the first tool in this chapter was developed to support practitioners, supervisors and managers to 'rumble with vulnerability' within the assessment and management of risk.

REFLECTIVE RISK MANAGEMENT TOOL

What is the tool?

The tool (Figure 1.1) helps individuals or groups to reflect on thoughts and feelings associated with their management of risk. Coupled with solution-oriented questioning, the tool can help to sensitively acknowledge and question individual

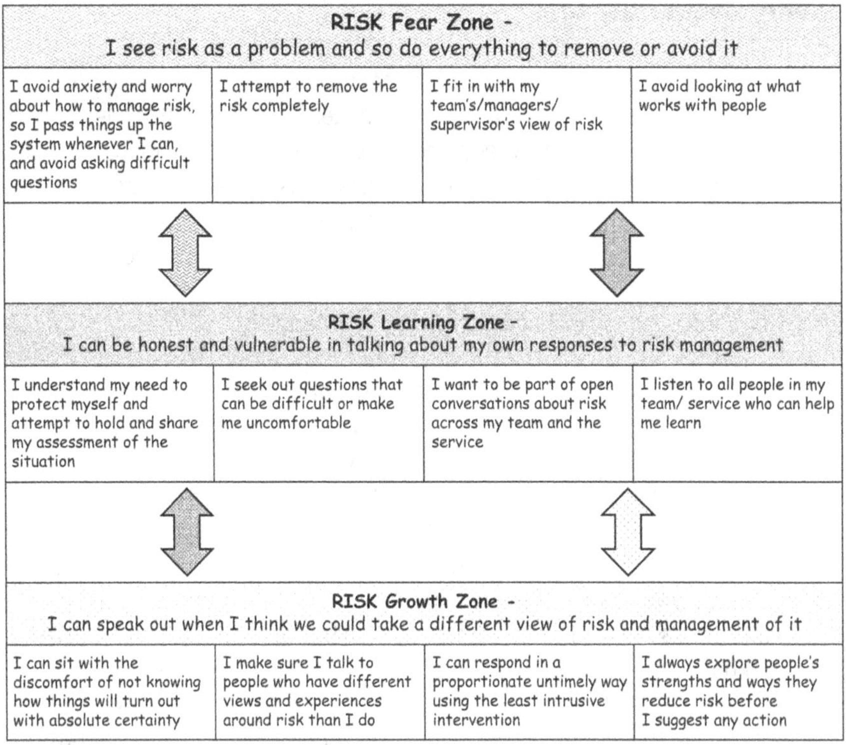

RISK Fear Zone - I see risk as a problem and so do everything to remove or avoid it			
I avoid anxiety and worry about how to manage risk, so I pass things up the system whenever I can, and avoid asking difficult questions	I attempt to remove the risk completely	I fit in with my team's/managers/ supervisor's view of risk	I avoid looking at what works with people

RISK Learning Zone - I can be honest and vulnerable in talking about my own responses to risk management			
I understand my need to protect myself and attempt to hold and share my assessment of the situation	I seek out questions that can be difficult or make me uncomfortable	I want to be part of open conversations about risk across my team and the service	I listen to all people in my team/ service who can help me learn

RISK Growth Zone - I can speak out when I think we could take a different view of risk and management of it			
I can sit with the discomfort of not knowing how things will turn out with absolute certainty	I make sure I talk to people who have different views and experiences around risk than I do	I can respond in a proportionate untimely way using the least intrusive intervention	I always explore people's strengths and ways they reduce risk before I suggest any action

Figure 1.1 Reflective Risk Management tool

and collective viewpoints, with the overall aim of improving children's and adults' wellbeing and safety. The tool can be used to support all professionals involved in managing situations where risk and complexity arise.

From my experience as a practice manager in a social work team, I've collaborated closely with early help services. I noticed that when people felt uncomfortable managing certain situations, they often wanted to pass them over to the social work team. This worry often halted progress and clouded their judgement. In my role as a practice development lead, this was seen more widely across all services. To address this, I teamed up with a colleague to create a tool that supports conversations and helps individuals consider other factors influencing their decisions. This tool encourages open dialogue and helps individuals gain confidence in their decision-making process. In addition, the tool includes statements for consideration to support the practitioner to notice where they are at that moment in time.

Theory behind the tool

The tool was developed holding in mind the optimum environment to support effective practice. The team as a Secure Base Model (Cook *et al.*, 2020) identifies five aspects needed to provide a secure team base for workers: team membership, availability, sensitivity, acceptance and cooperation. This concept is affirmed within The Social Work Organisational Resilience Diagnostic tool (Grant and Kinman, 2021) and confirms competent risk assessment and management is achieved through a culture of organisational resilience and a strong commitment to maintaining values, building trust and managing change and uncertainty.

Managing risk and interpersonal dynamics in uncertain situations can be challenging as achieving a definitive outcome is often difficult due to the numerous variables involved with human behaviour. The concept of working with uncertainty safely developed by Barry Mason (1993, cited in Funded by the Department for Education PSDP-Resources and Tools: Safe uncertainty 2 Practice Tool: Safe uncertainty, n.d.) suggests that as human beings we seek a level of certainty which increases our feelings of safety. However, Mason also suggests that this at times can be stifling and limit growth. For example, if we imagine a baby who is pulling themselves up to a standing position using the furniture, as a parent we may be fearful that the child will fall back and hit their head and step in to stop this, and if we do, it is very unlikely that the child will build the strength and co-ordination to stand, walk and in the long term run. We, therefore, assess the risk of the likelihood the child may lose their balance and fall backwards and put in measures to lessen the impact if they do. The model of safe uncertainty is built on the concept 'that for useful change to happen we sometimes need to become less certain of the positions we hold' (p. 4). If we maintain a position of curiosity, rather than a fixed view of certainty, we are more likely to be open to hearing other people's views and receptive to other possibilities.

To promote the concept of curiosity, the **Reflective Risk Management** tool is underpinned by a set of solution-oriented questions to promote self-reflection, awareness and change. Solution-oriented practice is not about denying the problems or challenges; it is about acknowledging them and identifying possibilities and potential outcomes (de Shazer, 1988). Through applying the questions of the tool, the object is to help colleagues notice times when they are successfully managing uncertainty and consider what contributes to their success, with the purpose that through noticing this, they will seek or do more of the same to improve practitioners' ability to manage risk alongside promoting positive health and wellbeing. A literature review conducted by Williams (2023) identified that there is a possible link between a practitioner's avoidant or dismissive style of attachment within supervision and a supervisee's emotional processing, case discussion, decision-making and wellbeing. Through using this tool, we are advocating for practitioners to acknowledge and accept their feelings, thereby supporting them to address their concerns.

Purpose

This tool can be used to support risk management through recognising our feelings and identifying personal and external existing strengths, which the practitioner can draw upon to support working with uncertainty safely. The tool can be used in supervision, individually, with another person, or in a group, to aid reflection.

Description

The tool is divided into zones, each containing several statements for the practitioner or colleague to reflect on their current feelings.

- ✓   There is no zone which is the wrong zone.
- ✓   Everyone experiences all the zones at different times.
- ✓   We must acknowledge how we/others feel and support the management of feelings and behaviours.
- ✓   You can be in more than one zone at a time.

Zones

This Risk Fear Zone signifies a high state of alertness, feeling overwhelmed, fear and panic. If a person is in the red zone, they may need to regulate, feel safe and gain control.

The Risk Learning Zone signifies a person may be open in their approach to risk management, showing willingness to learn, communicate and address challenging issues.

The Risk Growth Zone is the optimum zone and represents a willingness and openness to consider alternative perspectives and to sit confidently with the uncomfortableness associated with safe uncertainty.

How to use the tool

Identify Your Zone: The practitioner considers their current approach to risk management and identifies the zone that best represents their current state.

⇨   Take a moment to reflect on your risk management in this situation, which zone would you place yourself in?

Self-Observation: The practitioner notices what indicates as to why they have chosen the zone.

⇨   What do you notice about yourself that tells you that you are in this zone?

External Observation: The practitioner considers what others might notice about them.

⇨   What would others notice?

Support Needs when in the Risk Fear Zone: If a person identifies they are in the red zone, consider what is needed for them to feel safe and regulated before proceeding. Ingra du Buisson-Narsai (2020) suggests this could be as simple as taking a deep breath, pausing purposefully to focus on the present moment, having a cup of tea or going for a walk. By asking the person what they need, you are acknowledging their feelings and seeking to understand how you can assist them, rather than imposing your own ideas of what should be done.

Questions to ask include the following:

⇨   What do you need at this moment to support you to feel safe, regulated and in control?
⇨   What has helped before?
⇨   You may pause the further questions until you have what you need.

When the person is ready, engaging in brief reflective practice exercises can help to slow down thinking, enhance learning and foster lasting change. By intentionally slowing down thoughts through self-reflection or reflective conversations, new neural pathways can develop and support wellbeing and decision-making (du Buisson-Narsai, 2020), ultimately supporting effective risk management.

Risk fear zone

Reflecting in the Risk Fear Zone involves acknowledge times when the practitioner has felt different. Here are some questions to aid reflection:

⇨ Think of a different time when you have been in a different zone – which zone was this and what was different about this time?

⇨ What else was different about this situation? You? Others around you?

⇨ When you feel at your best, what do you notice about yourself?

⇨ What do you notice about what is around you that contributes to this?

⇨ What difference does this make to you?

⇨ What difference does this make to others?

⇨ From taking this time to reflect what are you going to pay attention to going forward?

⇨ What do you need around you to do this?

⇨ How will you let people around you know how you are feeling and what you need?

⇨ How will you know that this is working for you and those people whom you make decisions for?

Risk learning zone

Reflecting in the Risk Learning Zone can be very insightful. Here are some questions that might help to reflect on risk management and identify areas for growth and improvement.

⇨ How do I assess and communicate my own risk levels?

⇨ What strategies do I use to protect myself in risky situations?

⇨ What difficult questions have I avoided, and why?

⇨ How can I become more comfortable with uncomfortable questions?

⇨ How often do I engage in open conversations about risk with my team?

⇨ What can I do to encourage more open discussions about risk?

⇨ Who in my team can provide valuable insights about risk management?

⇨ How can I better listen and learn from my team members?

From taking this time to reflect what are you going to pay attention to going forward?

Risk growth zone

Reflecting in the Risk Growth Zone can be valuable. Here are some questions that might help you reflect on your approach to risk management and identify strengths in this area and identify potential areas for growth and improvement.

⇨ How do I feel about not knowing the outcomes with absolute certainty?

⇨ What strategies can I use to become more comfortable with uncertainty?

⇨   Who can I talk to that has different views and experiences around risk?

⇨   How can I ensure I am open to and respectful of these different perspectives?

⇨   How do I determine the most proportionate and timely response to a situation?

⇨   What are some examples of using the least intrusive intervention effectively?

⇨   What strengths and risk-reduction methods do I see in others before suggesting actions?

⇨   How can I better explore and acknowledge these strengths in my team?

⇨   From taking this time to reflect what are you going to pay attention to going forward?

Dilemmas, contradictions and uncertainty are pervasive features of social work practice (Egan et al., 2017, cited in Beddoe et al., 2022). The **Reflective Risk Management** tool provides opportunities to critically question, and process emotions associated with risk management.

The tool in practice

I have used this tool in several situations, including on myself, to support others in supervision and as a training activity. A particularly notable time was during a support session for a group of six practitioners who were struggling to agree on the level of support to provide to a family. The differing views had contributed to a position of blame and disconnect between the workers, to the extent that the parent was noticing this, and this division was distracting energy from the family's needs.

Using the tool in this context was powerful, as an independent facilitator with no designated authority within the casework, through the reflective approach facilitated by the tool, I promoted a sense of psychological safety within the group. By establishing the group's needs and developing agreements for how the group will work together, we established a productive and open environment wherein coworkers could share their views without feeling or being judged. Once we had identified and acknowledged which zone people were experiencing, we recognised that potentially all the professionals were closed off to others' views and were mostly in the Risk Fear and Risk Learning Zones. After this acceptance as a group, we spent time considering what each person would need to feel confident in the collective decision about the support for the family.

It was apparent that the breakdown in communication between the professionals resulted in the family's situation, and particularly the changes they had already made, having been overlooked. Through valuing each person's zone positions, the groups were able to support each other to feel fully informed to collectively agree on a way forward with the family.

This is one example of using this tool; I have also used it in my role as a practice educator to support conversations with a student who was struggling with the direction from the manager. The student was directed to close the case, using the tool identified that the student was fluctuating through the zones, fearful that ending the intervention would increase the risk but willing to take on board experienced practitioners' perspectives and ask questions to expand their knowledge, this supported them to expand their professional curiosity and sit comfortably within the space of safe uncertainty.

SUMMARY

This versatile tool can be used within supervision, to reflect individually or with others and in group settings. The tool successfully supports the practitioner to acknowledge their feelings and through using the reflective questions notice times when they have felt able to work with uncertainty safely. Developing a culture where people can voice how they are feeling is essential to improving practitioners' wellbeing and management of risk.

CONCERN AND STRENGTHS MATRICES TOOL

Inspiration

The idea for the **Concern and Strengths Matrices** *Tables 1.1 and 1.2 emerged from a blend of professional experiences and a passion for enhancing social work practices. Inspired by Turnell's Signs of Safety model (Turnell and Edwards, 1999). I aimed to create tools that assist practitioners in addressing concerns while emphasising strengths. The Concerns Matrix has been adapted from Turnell's original version and expands on the original set of questions to ensure a holistic perspective of the situation is established. This adaptation also ensures a strengths-based and safety-focused approach to safeguarding and social work, complemented by the addition of the Strengths Matrix. I remember a particular family's situation where a child's safety was at risk, and the use of these matrices helped to identify not only the critical concerns but also the strengths within the family and their network that could be leveraged to create a safer environment.*

This experience reinforced my belief in the importance of a balanced approach that considers both risks and strengths.

Introduction

The **Concern Matrix** and the **Strengths Matrix** are structured tools designed to help social workers and other professionals systematically identify, assess, and prioritise risks and concerns, as well as recognise and leverage strengths. It helps social workers systematically address concerns that could impact a child's or adults' safety and wellbeing. These tools are particularly useful in social work settings where understanding the severity and impact of various concerns, alongside the strengths and resources available, is crucial for effective intervention and support. The primary purpose of these matrices is to provide a comprehensive framework for evaluating concerns by considering their duration, history, impact, and associated challenges, while also identifying and leveraging strengths. These tools help professionals gather detailed information, analyse the situation, and assess both immediate and future risks and strengths. By doing so, they ensure that all relevant factors are considered, leading to more informed and effective decision-making.

Importance of detailed assessment in social work

When assessing a situation, it is crucial to gather specific, detailed information about the harm caused and its impact on the child, adult or others involved. The **Concern and Strengths Matrices** are designed to assist professionals to gather detailed information from other professionals or referrers. Alongside this, exploring existing strengths that mitigate against the concern is also essential.

Reasons for assessing both concerns and strengths

Assessing both concerns and strengths in social work is crucial for several reasons, as identified by Cailes et al. (2023):

- **Identifying Risks and Challenges**: Helps in understanding the immediate and potential threats to a child's or adult's wellbeing.
- **Recognising Individual Strengths and Resources**: Provides a fuller picture of their capabilities and resilience.

Table 1.1 Concern Matrix tool

Concern Matrix	How long has the concern been happening for?	When was the first time?	When was the worst time?	When was the most recent time?
What's happened or is happening? What are the challenges? What are other sources of information telling us?				
What is the impact of this? Describe the impact on the child, adult and others				
What makes the situation more difficult to manage/resolve?				
What happened in the past that may make the situation more difficult to resolve?				
What sets things off? What are the triggers and stressors?				

(Continued)

Table 1.1 *(Continued)*

Concern Matrix	How long has the concern been happening for?	When was the first time?	When was the worst time?	When was the most recent time?
What are the wider social or cultural factors that need to be considered?				
What will happen if things do not improve?				
Immediate concern What could be the worst thing that could happen if nothing changes?				
Future concern What will the future look like in 5/10/15 years if nothing changes?				
What risks are associated if change occurs?				

Table 1.2 Strength Matrix tool

Strengths Matrix	What are the strengths in relation to the concern? What are the individuals' strengths?	How is this situation already being effectively managed?	Times when this hasn't been a concern. (instances and exceptions) What were you doing? What were others doing?	What and who else makes the situation easier to manage? What are the external factors that reduce or increase the concern?
Current Situation: Description, including timeframe				
Triggers and Stressors: Description				
Social or cultural factors: Description				
Impact: Describe the difference this makes to the child, adult or others.				
Future strengths and wellbeing What is the outcome you're aiming for, what would be happening instead of the concern?				
Immediately				
Longer term				

- **Tailoring Interventions**: Understanding the concerns allows social workers to tailor interventions to address specific tasks.
- **Engagement with Change**: People who use services are more likely to engage with change when they feel their strengths are acknowledged.
- **Preventing Escalation**: Identifying existing strengths can help mitigate and contribute to preventing the situation from escalating.

Challenges with strengths-based approaches

Some practitioners feel uneasy with the increased autonomy and responsibility that comes with utilising strengths-based approaches, particularly when there is insufficient support from the organisation. Without this practitioners can feel anxious and resistant to adopting a strengths-based approach (Cailes et al., 2003) which can lead to defensive practice. Dominelli (2009) has extensively explored social work, highlighting the importance of addressing risks and the complexities involved in practice. Managing risk in social work requires not only identifying potential dangers but also understanding the ethical implications of interventions. Effective risk assessment involves

- **Engaging with People Who Use Services**: Understanding their perspectives and empowering them to participate in decision-making.
- **Maintaining Detailed Records**: Ensuring accountability and providing a clear rationale for decisions made.

These tools are designed to help social workers and colleagues explore detailed aspects of assessments. Determining the timeframe or severity of a concern can often be missing from risk assessments and assessing both the impact and the timeframe is crucial. If an issue occurred months ago with no recent episodes, it likely poses less risk now. Many concerns lack a clear timeframe, but upon investigation, they may be found to be outdated, reducing their urgency. Understanding the severity of harm and its impact helps prioritise which issues require immediate attention and resources.

Our brains are naturally inclined to focus on risks rather than identifying strengths, a concept known as negativity bias. This bias is well-documented in psychological research, showing that we tend to pay more attention to negative events and information than positive ones. The tool is a way to remind practitioners to explore the strengths in the situation and consider the difference these make to the identified concern.

How to use the concern and strengths matrices with people who use services

Using these matrices involves several key steps:

1   **Identify the Concern:**

   • Determine how long the concern has been happening, when it first occurred, the worst instance and the most recent occurrence.
   • Describe the specific events and challenges associated with the concern.

2   **Gather Information:**

   • Collect data from various sources such as network member views, observations, records and reports from other professionals.
   • Evaluate and describe the impact of the concern on the child, adult and others involved.

3   **Analyse the Situation:**

   • Identify what makes the situation difficult to manage or resolve.
   • Consider past events that may complicate the current situation.
   • Identify triggers and stressors, as well as any wider social or cultural factors.

4   **Assess Immediate and Future Risks:**

   • Determine the worst possible outcome if nothing changes.
   • Predict what the future might look like in 5, 10 or 15 years if the situation remains unchanged.
   • Outline risks associated with any potential changes.

5   **Identify and Leverage Strengths:**

   • Recognise times when the concern was less severe and identify supportive elements.
   • Consider external factors that influence the concern positively.
   • Identify the strengths of the individuals involved and how these can be leveraged to manage the situation.

Using the tools as conversation aids

The **Concern and Strengths Matrices** can also be used as conversation tools with the people who use services. By involving the person in the process, professionals can

- **Enhance Engagement**: Engaging them in discussions about their concerns and strengths can increase their involvement and commitment to the intervention process.
- **Empower People Who Use Services**: Support them to share their perspective and contribute to the assessment that helps empower them and ensures their voice is heard.
- **Build Trust**: Using the tools in a conversational manner can help build trust and rapport between the professional and the person.
- **Gather Comprehensive Information**: Direct conversations with the person can provide valuable insights and detailed information that might not be captured through other means.
- **Notice the Situation and Strengths**: Helping the person to notice and articulate their situation and the strengths associated with it can foster a deeper understanding and appreciation of their own resilience and resources.

By involving people who use services in the assessment process, professionals can create a more accurate, respectful and effective plan of action that truly addresses the client's needs and leverages their strengths. This collaborative approach not only enhances the quality of the intervention but also fosters a sense of partnership and mutual respect.

Introduction to Sarah's situation: Hoarding behaviour and self-neglect

Here is an example of how the matrix can be used with Sarah and her network of support: Tables 1.3 and 1.4.

Background and initial assessment

Sarah's hoarding behaviour and self-neglect had been ongoing for some time.

Detailed interventions

1   Initial Engagement and Trust-Building:

- **Initial Visit**: The social worker conducted an initial home visit to understand the extent of Sarah's hoarding and to build rapport. During this visit, the social worker listened empathetically to Sarah's

Table 1.3 Concern Matrix tool example

Concern Matrix Sarah's Hoarding Behaviour and Self-Neglect	How long has the concern been happening for?	When was the first time?	When was the worst time?	When was the most recent time?
What's happened or is happening? What are the challenges? What are other sources of information telling us?	Approximately 10 years (since 2014). Sarah collects and keeps items that most people would consider unnecessary, such as old newspapers, broken appliances and expired food.	After the death of Sarah's husband in 2014. Sarah begun to feel, overwhelmed with the responsibility of caring for herself and her home.	When her living room became completely inaccessible due to clutter in 2020. Her home is cluttered to the point where it poses safety risks, including fire hazards and limited mobility. Sarah has tripped over a pile of newspapers hurt her ankle, which required medical support from the hospital.	A minor fire hazard caused by accumulated papers near the kitchen stove in October 2024.
What is the impact of this? Describe the impact on the child, adult and others	Sarah is worried about the cost of professional cleaning services if things get worse. My children have mentioned the possibility of eviction if my home is deemed unsafe, which adds to my stress and financial worries.	Sarah says, 'The clutter is overwhelming. Every time I look at it, I feel anxious and stressed. It's a constant reminder of how much I must manage, and it makes my grief over losing my husband even harder to bear'.	Sarah says, 'it is hard to move around safely. I haven't invited anyone over in years because I'm embarrassed about the state of my home. I feel ashamed and isolated, which makes me even more depressed and lonely'.	Sarah's family has said they are afraid to visit because of the clutter. They worry about tripping or getting hurt. This means I see them less often, which makes me feel even more alone. Sarah's neighbours are worried that the next fire could be worse and spread to their home.

(Continued)

Table 1.3 (Continued)

Concern Matrix Sarah's Hoarding Behaviour and Self-Neglect	How long has the concern been happening for?	When was the first time?	When was the worst time?	When was the most recent time?
What makes the situation more difficult to manage/resolve?				
What happened in the past that may make the situation more difficult to resolve?	Sarah's emotional attachment to her possessions and her resistance to discarding items. The clutter makes it difficult for her to move around safely and maintain a clean-living environment. Sarah's hoarding behaviour intensified after her husband's death in 2014, suggesting a link to grief and loss. Sarah has said that as a child her family were poor, and she had to make do with hand me downs from her sisters. Her parents often struggled to provide enough food for everyone. Sarah says she was sometimes hungry.			
What sets things off? What are the triggers and stressors?	Sarah says she feels lonely and is worried about losing memories associated with her possessions. When people tell her to do something about it, she says she doesn't want to do what they tell her as no one understands. Sarah says the task is too big.			
What are the wider social or cultural factors that need to be considered?	There is a stigma around hoarding in Sarah's community, which makes her reluctant to seek help. The community are losing patience and worried about their own safety. They are worried about the potential infestation of rats in the community.			

(Continued)

Table 1.3 (Continued)

Concern Matrix Sarah's Hoarding Behaviour and Self-Neglect	How long has the concern been happening for?	When was the first time?	When was the worst time?	When was the most recent time?
What will happen if things do not improve?				
Immediate concern What could be the worst thing that could happen if nothing changes?		If the situation continues, Sarah could face serious health risks, including the danger of tripping and falling, the risk of fires and even the possibility of being asked to leave her home because it's not safe to live in. She will continue to feel lonely and not see her family and friends.		
Future concern What will the future look like in 5/10/15 years if nothing changes?		If the hoarding continues over the next 5–10 years, Sarah's living conditions could get much worse. This could lead to more health problems and make her feel even more isolated from friends and family.		
What risks are associated if change occurs?		Introducing changes to Sarah's living environment might initially increase her anxiety and resistance. She has said she wants to make changes at her own pace.		

Table 1.4 Strength Matrix tool example

Strengths Matrix	What are the strengths in relation to the concern? What are the individuals' strengths?	How is this situation already being effectively managed?	Times when this hasn't been a concern. (instances and exceptions) What were you doing? What were others doing?	What and who else makes the situation easier to manage? What are the external factors that reduce the concern?
Current Situation: Description, including timeframe	Sarah has a strong attachment to her home and a desire to preserve memories, which can be redirected towards creating a safer environment.	Sarah says, she has days, where she is motivated and tries to clear a small area.	Sarah managed to keep her home tidy when her husband was alive, indicating she has the capability to maintain a clean environment under different circumstances.	Sarah's adult children are supportive and willing to help. They came last year and attempted to help Sarah; they want things to get better for her. Her social worker is experienced in dealing with people who hoard belongings.
Triggers and stressors: Description	Sarah wants to feel less isolated and spend time with her family. She phoned her daughter and told her, she wants things to be different (Oct 24).	Sarah has started attending therapy (Nov 2024) sessions to address her grief and anxiety, although progress is slow.	Sarah says she felt more in control last year but things have slipped again.	Sarah's therapist A local support group for individuals with hoarding behaviour. This has helped Sarah to feel like she is not alone; she has said she realises other people like to keep things too.

(Continued)

Table 1.4 (*Continued*)

Strengths Matrix	What are the strengths in relation to the concern? What are the individuals' strengths?	How is this situation already being effectively managed?	Times when this hasn't been a concern. (instances and exceptions) What were you doing? What were others doing?	What and who else makes the situation easier to manage? What are the external factors that reduce the concern?
Social or cultural factors: Description	The neighbours check in with Sarah, through listening for movement in her home, they have contacted Jenny, Sarah's daughter, when they have been worried.	The local community church group have offered to clear Sarah's garden up and remove the rubbish from outside.	Sarah was part of the church group; she last visited the church last year. She found the people, so kind and friendly.	Local community church Group The fire service has completed a fire safety audit.
Impact: Describe the difference this makes to the child, adult or others.	When Sarah meets with people, she says she feels supported by her friends, family and local community, as well as professionals. She has said she has hope that things can get better.			

(Continued)

Table 1.4 (Continued)

Strengths Matrix	What are the strengths in relation to the concern? What are the individuals' strengths?	How is this situation already being effectively managed?	Times when this hasn't been a concern. (instances and exceptions) What were you doing? What were others doing?	What and who else makes the situation easier to manage? What are the external factors that reduce the concern?
Future strengths and wellbeing	What is the outcome you're aiming for, what would be happening instead of the concern?			
Immediately	Sarah and her friends and family want her home safer and cleaner by reducing clutter in key areas. Everyone has agreed to focus on clearing out the living room, kitchen and bathroom first. These areas will be tidy and free from too many items, making it easier for Sarah to move around safely and reducing any fire risks. Sarah will keep her important belongings and together, with her family will decide what to keep, what to donate and what to throw away.			
Longer term	Sarah will be living in a safer and more comfortable home; she will feel connected to her family and friends and enjoy spending time with them in her home; she will feel better overall because she has more control over her space and feelings, making life a lot easier and more enjoyable. Sarah will have an understanding why she likes to keep things, that are no longer needed. Sarah will have new ways to cope with these feelings without holding onto too many things. Over time, she will be helped to organise her entire home. Each room will have a place for everything, and everyone will make sure it stays clean and clutter-free. Sarah's home will be a comfortable and safe place to live.			

story, acknowledging her grief and the emotional attachment to her possessions.

- **Building Trust**: Over several visits, the social worker continued to build trust by showing genuine concern for Sarah's wellbeing and avoiding judgemental language. This helped Sarah feel more comfortable and open to discussing her situation.

2 **Assessment Using the Concern Matrix**:

- **Identifying Concerns**: The social worker used the Concern Matrix to document the duration, history and impact of Sarah's hoarding. This included noting the worst instance in 2020 when her living room became completely inaccessible and the most recent incident involving a minor fire hazard in October 2024.
- **Gathering Information**: Information was gathered from various sources, including Sarah's family, neighbours and medical records. This comprehensive assessment highlighted the physical and emotional impact of the hoarding on Sarah and her family.
- **Identifying Strengths**: The social worker used the Strengths Matrix to recognise times when the concern was less severe and identify supportive elements, including external factors that influence the concern positively as well as identify the strengths of the individuals involved and how these can be leveraged to manage the situation.

Sarah's case highlights the importance of a comprehensive approach that addresses both the concerns and strengths in her situation. By leveraging her support network and focusing on achievable goals, there is hope for significant improvement in her quality of life.

This matrix provides a structured approach to understanding and addressing Sarah's hoarding behaviour, focusing on both the concerns and strengths in her situation.

Evaluating strengths and weaknesses using the concern and strengths matrices

The next step is to take time to analyse the situation. Evaluating strengths and weaknesses using the Concern and Strengths Matrices involves a systematic approach to understanding both the positive attributes and potential areas for improvement in a person's situation. Here are the key steps tailored to these matrices:

1   **Identify Strengths:**

- **Concern Matrix**: Recognise times when the concern was less severe and identify supportive elements that contributed to these periods. This helps in understanding the individual's resilience and coping mechanisms.
- **Strengths Matrix**: List the strengths that are directly relevant to the concern, such as personal qualities, skills and resources. For example, a supportive family or a favourite calming activity can be significant strengths.

2   **Identify Weaknesses**:

- **Concern Matrix**: Identify what makes the situation difficult to manage or resolve. This includes understanding the triggers, stressors and past events that complicate the current situation.
- **Strengths Matrix**: Recognise areas where the individual or situation lacks resources or support. This can include identifying times when the concern was more severe and understanding what factors contributed to these challenges.

3   **Analyse Context**:

- **Concern Matrix**: Consider the wider social or cultural factors that need to be considered. This helps in understanding the broader context of the concern and its impact on the individual.
- **Strengths Matrix**: Analyse how external factors, such as the environment or cultural expectations, influence the concern. This helps in leveraging these factors to support the individual.

4   **Assess Risks and Strengths:**

- **Concern Matrix**: This includes determining the worst possible outcome if nothing changes and predicting future concerns.
- **Strengths Matrix**: This includes recognising supportive elements and understanding how the situation is currently being managed successfully.

5   **Set Goals and Develop Plans**:

- **Concern Matrix**: Based on the evaluation, set realistic goals for addressing the concerns. Develop action plans that include specific steps and resources needed for improvement.
- **Strengths Matrix**: Set goals for leveraging strengths to mitigate concerns. Develop plans that focus on enhancing the individual's resilience and coping mechanisms.

6   **Monitor and Review**:

- **Concern Matrix**: Continuously monitor progress and adjust as needed. Regularly review the assessment to reflect changes and new insights.
- **Strengths Matrix**: Regularly review and update the strengths assessment to ensure that the support provided remains relevant and effective.

By following these steps, social workers and other professionals can conduct thorough and effective evaluations of strengths and weaknesses using the Concern and Strengths Matrices. This approach ensures that all relevant factors are considered, leading to better outcomes for people who use services by addressing both their risks and leveraging their strengths.

I have also used this tool during a professional meeting with practitioners who had different views on the severity of a child's missing episodes. The tools helped extract information about the timeframe of the missing episodes and explore existing safety measures to reduce them.

Summary

The **Concern and Strengths Matrices** are invaluable tools for social workers and other professionals in systematically identifying, assessing and addressing both risks and strengths in their practice. By providing a structured framework, these matrices ensure that all relevant factors are considered, leading to more informed and effective decision-making.

The Concern Matrix helps in pinpointing potential threats to a child's or adult's safety and wellbeing, while the Strengths Matrix focuses on recognising and leveraging individual and contextual strengths. This balanced approach not only aids in managing risks but also empowers service users by highlighting their capabilities and resources. Incorporating these tools into practice fosters a collaborative and empowering environment, where people who use services are actively involved in the assessment process. This engagement builds trust and rapport, making interventions more relevant and effective. Additionally, these matrices serve as valuable aids for self-reflection, helping professionals to continuously improve their practice and maintain high standards of care. Ultimately, the use of the **Concern and Strengths Matrices** promotes a holistic and strengths-based approach to social work, ensuring that interventions are not only responsive to immediate risks but also supportive of long-term resilience and wellbeing.

Three key points

1 **Balance risks and strengths:**

   • When you're looking at a situation, it's important to balance spotting the risks with recognising the strengths. Sure, you need to know what could go wrong, but don't forget to highlight what's going right. This balanced view helps create better plans and makes people feel more capable and resilient.

2 **Engage and empower people who use services:**

   • Get the people you're helping involved in the process. When they share their thoughts and take part in the assessment, it builds trust and makes them more likely to stick with the plan. This teamwork approach ensures the support is relevant and respectful of their unique needs.

3 **Continuous reflection and adaptation:**

   • Keep reflecting on your work and be ready to adapt. When we feel able to express how we are feeling without fear of judgement, we can work towards a different outcome. Knowing your own strengths and areas for improvement helps you grow and stay effective in your role. Continuous learning and adapting are key to providing the best care and support.

REFERENCES

Beddoe, L. *et al.* (2022) 'Supervision in child protection: A space and place for reflection or an excruciating marathon of compliance?', *European Journal of Social Work*, 25(3), pp. 525–537. doi:10.1080/13691457.2021.1964443

Brown, B. (2018) *Dare to lead*. New York: Random House.

Cailes, J., Preston-Shoot, M. and Braye, S. (2023). *Self-neglect and safeguarding: A review of practice and policy*. Dartington: Research in Practice.

Cook, L.L., Zschomler, D., Biggart, L. and Carder, S. (2020) 'The team as a secure base revisited: Remote working and resilience among child and family social workers during COVID-19', *Journal of Children's Services*, (ahead-of-print). https://doi.org/10.1108/jcs-07-2020-0031

Department for Education. (2023) *Children's Social Care National Framework Statutory Guidance on the purpose, Principles for Practice and Expected Outcomes of children's Social Care*. [online] Available at: https://assets.publishing.service.gov.uk/media/657c538495bf650010719097/Children_s_Social_Care_National_Framework__December_2023.pdf. Accessed 2 February 2025.

Department of Health and Social Care. (2024) *Care and Support Statutory Guidance*. Available at: https://www.gov.uk/government/publications/care-act-statutory-guidance/care-and-support-statutory-guidance. Accessed 1 November 2024.

de Shazer, S. (1988) *Clues: Investigating solutions in brief therapy*. New York: W.W. Norton & Company.

Dixon, J. (2023) *Adult safeguarding observed: How social workers assess and manage risk and uncertainty*. Bristol: University Press.

Dominelli, L. (2009) *Introducing social work*. Cambridge: Polity Press.

du Buisson-Narsai, I. (2020) *Fight, flight or flourish: How neuroscience can unlock human potential*. Johannesburg: KR Publishing.

Egan, G. (2017) *The skilled helper: A problem-management and opportunity-development approach to helping*. 11th edn. Boston, MA: Cengage Learning.

Funded by the Department for Education PSDP-Resources and Tools: Safe uncertainty 2 Practice Tool: Safe uncertainty. (n.d.). Available at: https://tce.researchinpractice.org.uk/wp-content/uploads/2023/02/Safe-uncertainty.pdf. Accessed 2 February 2025.

Grant, L. and Kinman, G. (2021). *The Social Work Organisational Resilience Diagnostic (SWORD) tool and workbook*. 2nd edn. Research in Practice. Available at: https://sword.researchin-practice.org.uk/media/xobpd3eq/sword-tool-workbook-2nd-edition-2021.pdf

HM Government (2023). *Working together to safeguard children statutory framework: Legislation relevant to safeguarding and promoting the welfare of children*. [online] HM Government. Available at: https://assets.publishing.service.gov.uk/media/65797f1e0467eb000d55f689/Working_together_to_safeguard_children_2023_-_statutory_framework.pdf. Accessed 2 February 2025.

MacAlister, J. (2022) *The Independent Review of Children's Social Care*. Published on 23 May 2022. Available at: https://www.gov.uk/government/publications/independent-review-of-childrens-social-care-final-report. Accessed 1 November 2024.

Mason, B., 1993. Towards positions of safe uncertainty. *Human Systems: The Journal of Systemic Consultation & Management*, 4(3–4), pp. 189–200.

Turnell, A. and Edwards, S. (1999) *Signs of safety: A solution and safety oriented approach to child protection*. New York; London: W.W. Norton.

Williams, J. (2023) 'Supervision as a secure base: The role of attachment theory within the emotional and psycho-social landscape of social work supervision', *Journal of Social Work Practice*, 37, pp. 309–323. https://doi.org/10.1080/02650533.2022.2089639.

Chapter 2

Exploring risk and safety when working with child sexual abuse

Aisha Howells

INTRODUCTION

In England and Wales, at least one in ten children are sexually abused before the age of 16 years old (Karsna and Kelly, 2021). However, research data only shows what is captured in official statistics. It is well known that the scale and prevalence of child sexual abuse (CSA) are likely to be much higher as it is often hidden and relies on secrecy. In social work, fewer children are being placed on child protection plans with the category of sexual abuse. Research identified that some local authorities did not record any concerns of sexual abuse across a whole year (Karsna and Bromley, 2024), whilst police data shows sexual abuse offences have increased year on year, alongside greater severity in offending and complexity for professionals working in the field (NPCC, 2022). This suggests that there is a growing and concerning disconnect between the landscape of CSA and the support and protection of children.

CSA is an area that needs to be spoken about. Research suggests that key professionals lack the confidence, knowledge and skills when working in fields such as CSA and miss opportunities to identify and respond in these situations (CSA Centre, 2022). There are often concerns in knowing what to say or do and practitioners are fearful of getting things wrong. It can also be a difficult area to think about and at times, there can be a focus towards alternative explanations. Practice has often been police-led to the point where Glinski (2019) suggests that social work has inadvertently adopted the 'beyond reasonable doubt' threshold in our work which presents a range of difficulties, whereas it is important to remember that the legal threshold for social work intervention is 'the balance of probabilities', which means more than 50/50. So, it may be helpful to start asking ourselves, on balance, are there concerns that a child is being harmed and a response is needed?

DOI: 10.4324/9781041054740-3

This chapter provides three innovative tools to help practitioners explore the emotive subject of CSA with greater confidence, insight and skills. Instead of fearing that they may get things wrong, the hope is for practitioners to shift towards thinking 'what if I am right?' about a situation and 'what do I need to know and do, to make the child safer?'. The aim is to equip social workers with a toolkit to manage and address risk in this difficult and complex area of social work. Put simply, the more understanding practitioners have, the more effective their disruption and prevention of CSA.

WHAT IS CHILD SEXUAL ABUSE?

The UK Government's statutory definition of CSA 'involves forcing or enticing a child or young person to take part in sexual activities, not necessarily involving a high level of violence, whether or not the child is aware of what is happening' and outlines that sexual abuse can involve different forms and contexts (HM Government, 2023, p. 162). Children and adults can sexually abuse children, with abuse occurring in intra- and extra-familial contexts and online. Child sexual exploitation is a form of CSA.

Sexual abuse is the most reported type of abuse, with most victims being female and the majority of abusers are male (Howells, 2023, p. 227). Almost half of sexual abuse takes place before victims are 11 years old and the most common form of sexual abuse is in and around the family, whilst child-on-child abuse and online CSA are increasing (NPCC, 2022). Although evidence suggests that much sexual abuse remains unreported, there are additional difficulties for children of marginalised communities to speak up about sexual abuse due to racist and cultural stereotyping (Hodger *et al.*, 2020). Harm is intrinsic to CSA and there are wide-ranging and long-lasting impacts, with no two individuals affected in the same way (Vera-Gray, 2023).

TOOL 1: CSA A–Z FLASHCARDS

Inspiration

As part of my PhD research, I interviewed mothers whose children were subject to child sexual abuse. Many of the mothers shared that the difference in overall experience for them was down to one singular professional. This was often felt to be luck that they had stumbled across this practitioner, rather than consistently available across the field. One mother said, 'I was very fortunate and very lucky that I had a particular connection with one worker to be able to get the support I needed. She was the first professional that spoke to me like a person, rather than a mum'. I then spoke with practitioners about what they needed in practice as a starting point when working in the field of CSA. And so, drawn from mothers' voices, practitioners' experiences and research, the flashcards were born.

Introduction

The **CSA A-Z Flashcards** are a 'one-stop shop' for practitioners to start to think about CSA and equip them with the knowledge and skills needed when faced with a situation potentially involving sexual abuse. The flashcards are prompts for practitioners to consider the range of skills needed within their interventions, the actions to be implemented and considerations to be given thought. A key idea is that the **CSA A-Z Flashcards** are designed as a way to be mindful that sexual abuse may be taking place and what practitioners need to know and do in this situation. The flashcards are simply starting points to drive more in-depth discussions (Figure 2.1).

Figure 2.1 Tool 1: CSA A–Z flashcards

Theory

Flashcards (Figures 2.2 and 2.3) are an effective study tool used in education. Typically aimed at supporting recall, they are commonly associated with memorisation. However, flashcards are widely implemented to achieve deeper

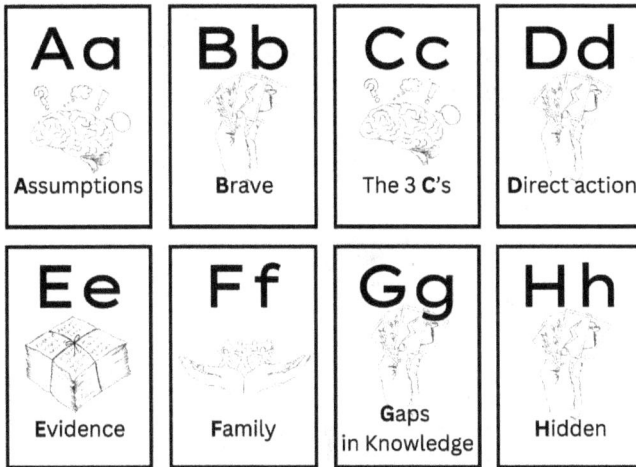

Aa	Bb	Cc	Dd
Assumptions	Brave	The 3 C's	Direct action
Ee	**Ff**	**Gg**	**Hh**
Evidence	Family	Gaps in Knowledge	Hidden

Figure 2.2 A–H of CSA A–Z flashcard set (front)

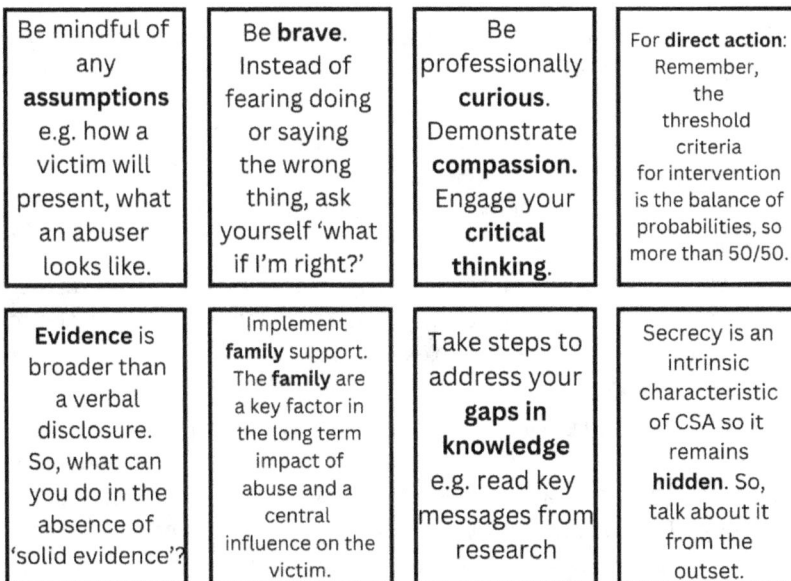

Be mindful of any **assumptions** e.g. how a victim will present, what an abuser looks like.	Be **brave**. Instead of fearing doing or saying the wrong thing, ask yourself 'what if I'm right?'	Be professionally **curious**. Demonstrate **compassion.** Engage your **critical thinking**.	For **direct action**: Remember, the threshold criteria for intervention is the balance of probabilities, so more than 50/50.
Evidence is broader than a verbal disclosure. So, what can you do in the absence of 'solid evidence'?	Implement **family** support. The **family** are a key factor in the long term impact of abuse and a central influence on the victim.	Take steps to address your **gaps in knowledge** e.g. read key messages from research	Secrecy is an intrinsic characteristic of CSA so it remains **hidden**. So, talk about it from the outset.

Figure 2.3 A–H of CSA A–Z flashcard set (back)

levels of understanding and application to topics (Senzaki *et al.*, 2017). Secondly, the flashcards are a tool which combines many different practice areas around CSA, which broadens professionals' understanding, helping them to make connections across the field, and embeds knowledge and skills for future practice. Finally, the flashcards also give practitioners an opportunity to step away from the computer and immerse themselves in a sensory experience.

For the entire CSA A-Z Flashcard set, please see appendices (available online via the Routledge book page).

How to use the tool

A suggestion is to print the flashcards on both sides and laminate them for longevity.

This is a tool that can be used individually, during one-to-one and peer supervision, or within a group setting e.g. Team Meeting. For example,

- Individually: The flashcards can be placed in a pile and explored methodically from A to Z alongside a presenting situation where there may be a concern or confirmed incident of sexual abuse.
- Supervision: The flashcards can be scattered and the practitioner chooses three to five cards to discuss with their peer(s) or supervisor, whilst thinking of a presenting scenario.
- Group: The practitioner presents the situation and members of the group offer their perspectives on a selection of their chosen flashcards to discuss together, to bring together their knowledge and expertise.

Another way to use the flashcards is to separate them into skills, considerations and actions, and focus discussion on the chosen area. There is no limit to how the flashcards can be used. So, feel free to experiment!

The tool was used in a group lecture with second-year students alongside a case study. The students worked in small groups, using the flashcards to channel their energies towards areas of priority and helped them start to make sense of the situation, consider their intervention strategies and key principles to guide their work. The students' feedback ranged from 'the cards helped me with my adaptability' to 'love these – will definitely use them in practice!'

Other ways to use the tool

This tool can be used between a practice educator and a learner within a supervision session to discuss different aspects of a situation involving CSA. Alternatively, the practice educator could set questions for the learner about different cards. For example, I = indicators – What are different indicators of sexual abuse and what can be seen in this presenting situation?, M = Holding different explanations in Mind – How can this situation be explained from a different perspective? What else might be going on?

TOOL 2: StoryStarters

Figure 2.4 Tool 2: StoryStarters
StoryStarters Illustration by Scarlet Howells

If you want a story with a happy ending, try another book ...

Few victims of CSA share what is happening to them at the time it is happening. So, practitioners should not respond by 'waiting' for a child to disclose but it is important, instead to identify possible signs and indicators of CSA and respond to a child in creative ways to understand what may be going on. Whatever the situation, with a child who may be spontaneously telling you about the abuse or if you have a suspicion, initial conversations about CSA can be difficult.

Child Safeguarding Practice Reviews (previously known as Serious Case Reviews (SCR)) which focus on improving learning from child deaths or in circumstances when a child is seriously harmed have highlighted how important it is that children remain at the core of any assessment or work. This means engaging with children in ways that help get to know them, understand their daily experiences and gain a sense of who they are. If a child has something distressing to share, it is likely they will speak to someone they know and trust the most. Although this may not always be a professional, this speaks to the significance of practitioners facilitating meaningful engagement with children in different ways. Remember, the child's welfare is paramount and research tells us that children need 'help to tell' (Glinski and Sabin, 2022). This suggests that practitioners need to create spaces where children have the opportunity to tell or, when something is wrong, are asked about it.

StoryStarters (Figure 2.4) are a tool which helps to convey to the child that the practitioner is showing an active interest in their life by listening to them and being professionally curious. Irrespective of the reasons practitioners are involved with a child, attempts to build a relationship can not only contribute towards showing them that their ideas, thoughts and feelings matter, but also help understand that the telling is a process.

There was a witch called Meg ...

When my daughter was younger, her favourite story was Meg and Mog, a book about a witch and her cat on their adventures. Firstly, I would read the book to her and then I'd go back to the start again, but this time I'd start the story about my daughter and let her tell me a story, in her own words. She would absolutely love this part and sometimes rushed me to the end, so she could start! I found this window into her world fascinating and it really helped me tune into her. Storytime also became an important family tradition for us and I came to realise the value of storytelling in the role it plays within children's lives. And so, 'Once upon a time, there was a witch called Ava ...'

This is how the story begins

The underpinning theory for the **StoryStarters** tool is narrative theory (Squire, Andrews and Tamboukou, 2013). Social work is narrative in nature with talking, interaction and storytelling of experiences being fundamental to practice (Baldwin, 2013; Riessman and Quinney, 2005). Social workers draw on narrative theory to make sense of people's experiences and are curious about the influences that shape storytelling practices. For example, through completion of assessments, reviews, presentations to panels and attendance at courts, which are, in essence, narrative activities. Here, in this **StoryStarters** activity, the child may tell a personal account or a series of stories framed through interactions by their audience e.g. you, the practitioner. This means your role is key and there are some tips below to remember. Storytelling also provides many educational and psychological benefits for children and can be a window to new worlds helping them cope with everyday life. Storytelling also helps children feel valued and fosters strong bonds between storyteller and the audience.

Once upon a time ...

1   IF I COULD FLY …
    Use this as a way to ask where the child would fly away to, with whom and what the person means to them. You could also explore the fun of a superpower and ask about special talents.
2   IF I GOT LOST …
    Use this as a way to ask about where the child's safe spaces are and who their trusted person is. You could also be curious about how they feel when making a mistake and their ability to problem solve.
3   TOMORROW WHEN I WAKE UP …
    Ask about what the child would want to be different. This allows exploration of a child's daily experiences and stepping into a reality where things could look and feel different. You could use metaphorical images such as a magic wand or crystal ball or ask 'tomorrow, when you wake up, you have a 10/10 day – what would this involve and how would it feel?'
4   I AM AN EXPLORER IN A MAGICAL KINGDOM …
    This can be helpful to find out what is important to the child when they are on a mission, how they may feel in an unknown land and how they behave when encountering obstacles. You could set the scene in different ways, from fantasy, in the wilderness, a Lego world or a way which resonates with the child. Once established in the kingdom, you could ask them about navigating dark tunnels, what guards the treasure and what every explorer needs to protect them.

5   IF THERE WAS A MAGICAL DOOR IN THE BACK OF MY WARDROBE …
Ask about the child moving between worlds. What these different worlds look and feel like. Ask about who or what are in the worlds. You can also explore due to the concealed nature of the passageway, their understanding and feelings towards secrets and secret keeping.

6   I AM A STRONG KNIGHT AND I FIND A MONSTER IN A DUNGEON …
Use this as a way to find out about the child's experiences of being brave or kind. You can ask about hard things they have done and what has helped them. You can also explore if the child is worried or scared by anything.

7   IF I HAD THE BEST DAY …
Ask about what makes the child happy. What do they like to do that makes them feel good about themselves. Ask about the child's favourite interests, hobbies and activities. You can then follow up with exploring if there is anything that makes them feel unhappy.

8   MY FAVOURITE TOY COMES TO LIFE …
What toy is it? Find out about the toy and meaning it holds for the child. Ask about what it would say and what they would do together.

9   I AM A BUBBLE FLOATING AWAY …
This can be a chance for a child to talk about any concerns. You can encourage children to imagine putting any worries inside a floating bubble. As the bubble is blown upwards, you can ask them to imagine any troubles moving out of their body, carried in their breath and captured by the bubble and floating out of their sight and leaving them. If the bubble pops, don't worry, this means the worries can also melt away too or try again until they float away.

10   IT IS WACKY WEDNESDAY …
Sometimes, it's important to be silly and laugh to strengthen relationships. Consider picking something that is out of place or is fun for the child. For example, place a sock over your hands or on the legs of chairs. Share that your elbow can speak and place googly eyes on the end. Say that you have to wear special glasses today and wear some pop out, springy eyes or mix the meanings of your words up, where 'yes' means 'no' and things are opposite. There is no limit to silliness!

To use the **StoryStarters** tool, consider the child's comfort and take steps to put the child at ease, act sensitively and find a location with privacy. Considerations may include whether the child prefers being outside, walking whilst talking or being inside with access to comforting toys. It will be helpful for you to get physically on the same level and complete this activity with the child alone if possible and remember to have congruence between your words and actions, displaying sensitivity, compassion and active listening. This activity may also involve adaptations for children with additional needs and will be dependent upon a child's communication needs and preferences.

It is important to note that the **StoryStarters** are ways to encourage interaction between the child and practitioner, help the child feel comfortable about sharing and can propel more exploration of the child's life. It will be key to ask more direct questions to clarify anything the child has shared that is of concern at the time or come back to, at a later time. You may wish to have some sensory objects or accompaniments to the **StoryStarters** tool for children to immerse themselves in the activity, such as the following:

1   Cape (IF I COULD FLY)
4   Explorer's hat (I AM AN EXPLORER IN A MAGICAL KINGDOM)
6   Toy sword (I AM A STRONG KNIGHT AND FIND A MONSTER IN A DUNGEON)
9   Bubbles (I AM A BUBBLE FLOATING AWAY)
10   Socks, springy or googly eyes (IT IS WACKY WEDNESDAY)

Glinski and Sabin (2022) outline three vital components in a child's experience of talking to someone about sexual abuse which will be helpful to keep in mind:

1   They are believed.
2   Action is taken to protect them.
3   Emotional support is provided.

In light of this, to accompany the tool is the following grid of example questions and responses on the next page (Table 2.1), which may help social workers in practice.

Safe? 'Course he isn't safe. But he's good

*When using the **StoryStarters** tool with Scarlet, a 7-year-old girl, I used the 'I am a bubble and I am floating away …' starter alongside giant bubble wands in the garden to huff and puff our bubbles away in the wind. She shared a list of her worries from dogs to insects, the dark, having tummy aches, death, natural disasters and the dark. I used her sharing of these, to propel inquisitive questions about what made her so frightened about these fears and why.*

TAP! TAP! Who's that?

The **StoryStarters** tool is child-focussed. However, this tool can be adapted to use between a practice educator and learner. Stories can be a good way to elicit information and a fun way in getting to know someone, particularly in the early stages of practice learning. It is also a good way to develop insight. The

Table 2.1 Grid of example questions and responses

Question/ response	Examples
Top tips	• An important aspect of this tool is to not interrupt or correct the child and use age-appropriate language. You will also need to factor in knowing when to stop asking questions, whilst not shutting the child down in any way. • Remain calm in your approach. • Be self-aware of your values, experiences and presenting behaviour towards a child.
Prompting questions	• Can you tell me more about that? • What else has happened that makes you feel …? • I notice that … • I can see that you are … • I wonder how you feel about … • Go on …
Clarifying questions	• Ask 'who, what, when, where', questions to obtain specific facts about the situation. • Children often use different words to describe things, can you tell me what you mean when you say …?
Validating responses	• What you have told me … has done is not okay. This should not have happened to you and was not your fault. • Sometimes people who hurt children tell them all sorts of things to make the child think they shouldn't tell anyone. • Adults/other children should never do these things to children. • I am here for you. You are not alone. • I believe you (depending on your role). • I will do everything I can to help keep you safe. • I can see how difficult this is for you. You have done everything you can.
Addressing power	• If I get something wrong, please tell me. • Is there anything else you want to tell me? • This is what will happen now … Is there anything you would like me to do, to help you?

practice educator and learner could complete the activity together, taking it in turns to share. One way would be to adapt the **StoryStarters**, for example,

1   I RECALL SOMEONE WHO HAD A PROFOUND IMPACT ON ME …
    Use this as a way to ask about who has influenced the learner's life, how and in what way.
2   IF I GOT LOST …
    Use this as a way to ask about the learner's safe spaces and who their trusted person is. You could also be curious about how they feel about making a mistake and their ability to problem solve.
3   TOMORROW WHEN I WAKE UP …
    Ask about what the learner would want to be different. This allows exploration of a learner's daily experiences and stepping into a reality where things could look and feel different. You could use metaphorical images such as a crystal ball, if this is helpful or ask 'Tomorrow, when you wake up, you have a 10/10 day – what would this involve and how would it feel?'
4   A SHIVER RACED DOWN MY SPINE AND A LUMP CAME TO MY THROAT …
    Use this as a way to ask what the learner is fearful of and why. You could explore what is holding them back and how things might change if they were able to overcome this fear.
5   THERE IS WARMTH IN THIS OLD MEMORY …
    Encourage the learner to reflect on a special memory, what it means to them and why it holds such value for them.
6   THERE IS MAGIC IN AN ORDINARY DAY OR MOMENT …
    Use this as a way to explore what aspects of a day-to-day routine or in a typical moment gives the learner joy. You could also elicit ways in which the learner finds magic or happiness in each day e.g. self-care, rituals, and what is important for them in their everyday.
7   THE HAPPIEST MOMENT IN MY LIFE …
    Ask about what makes the learner happy. What do they like to do that makes them feel good about themselves. Ask about the learner's favourite interests, hobbies and activities. You can then follow up with exploring if there is anything that makes them feel unhappy.
8   I WOULD LIKE TO BE REMEMBERED …
    Use this as a way to ask what guides the learner's daily life. This is essentially an exploration of the learner's values, what they stand for and how they show up in life. You may ask an additional question of 'how do you want to make people feel?', which can lend itself to further discussions in their professional practice with people with lived experience.

9   A TRADITION FROM MY CULTURE …
Ask about the tradition's personal significance to the learner and what this means to them and why. This also allows sharing of whether the learner participates in the custom, the history and practice.

10   I FAILED AN EXAM ONCE …
Reflecting on situations which involve personal setbacks can help learners understand their feelings, experiences and consequences of failures. They can be encouraged to think critically about the lessons they have learnt and what contributes to their understanding of failing and the steps to reframe, learn and develop.

TOOL 3: CSA HIGHER ORDER THINKING TOOL

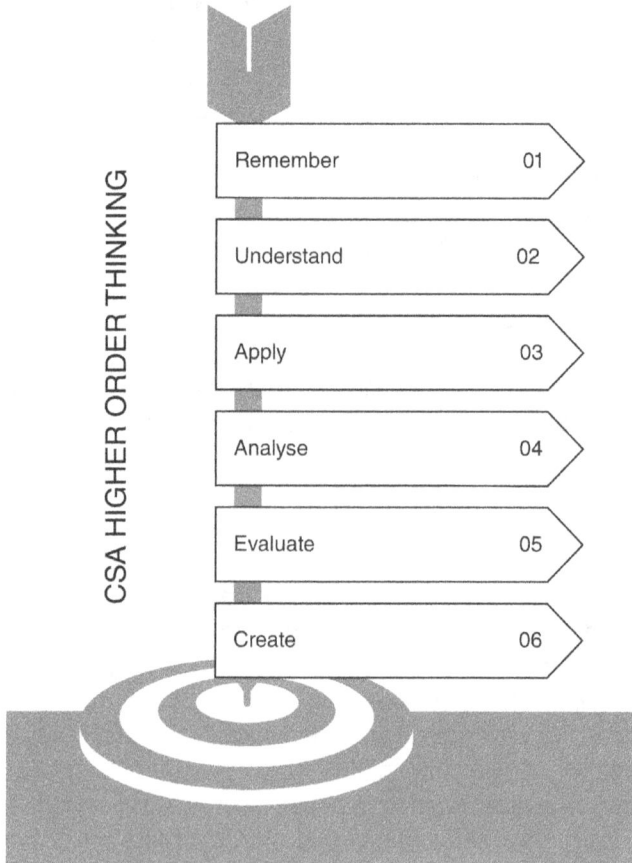

Figure 2.5 Tool 3: CSA higher order thinking tool

Inspiration

As a lecturer at a university with a research interest in child sexual abuse, I am always keen to develop students' understanding and critical thinking in this field particularly given it is an issue that they may experience in placement or as a qualified social worker. A key area that we touch on is the tension between following processes and procedures without question, alongside the need for critical thinking. Critical thinking requires practitioners to 'step outside of themselves' and allows creativity to flourish, whilst procedural guidance maintains focus towards the status quo and is known to not be conducive to such thinking. Critical thinking is the heart of practice, and this tool was developed to help cultivate deliberative thinking in this area.

Introduction

Effective critical thinking is integral to social work practice. However, concerns exist about the quality of practitioners' critical thinking and analytical skills (Munro, 2011). There are different components which enable critical thinking such as the identification and challenge of assumptions, exploring the importance of context and holding different explanations in mind (Brookfield, 1997). Critical thinking also requires practitioners to be brave to interrogate ourselves and develop understanding of how we know what we know. It is a lesson in humility to question ourselves, deepen our understanding and grow. The **CSA Higher Order Thinking** tool (Figure 2.5) provides the practitioner with support of their autonomy in learning about CSA and promotes a more thorough understanding of such a complex issue. The tool can inspire practitioners to engage with the difficult topic of CSA, rather than ignoring it. It is well-known that emotions are inherent to our decision-making (see Chapters 1 and 5) and critical thinking encourages us to consider our feelings, question our knowledge base and uncover the influences which shape how we understand the world around us. This is of particular importance, given the emotionally charged field of CSA which can impact a practitioner's sense of identity, values and beliefs, whilst strong emotional reactions can also become obstacles in the learning process. The aim of this tool is to preserve a practitioner's intrinsic motivation to explicitly engage with a sensitive topic such as childhood sexual abuse in a structured and thoughtful manner.

Theory

The **CSA Higher Order Thinking** tool is underpinned by Bloom's Taxonomy framework (1956) which categorises different levels of learning and thinking. As an influential model within education, it provides a guide for a hierarchical order of cognitive level skills for effective learning, ranging in complexity from recall to expertise and proficiency. Put simply, with the use of different tiers, the model helps us understand the process of learning and consider how knowledge is acquired and applied. Although there are criticisms of the framework that speak of a lack of imaginative understanding amongst others (Ormell, 1974), it can be a helpful way to not shy away from thinking in situations involving CSA and can help to cultivate critical thinking and problem-solving skills.

How to use the tool

The **CSA Higher Order Thinking** tool can be used individually or in supervision as a framework to remember, understand, apply, analyse, evaluate and create new learning within a situation involving a concern of CSA. The practitioner considers the six sections, moving from 'Level 01 Remember' to 'Level 06 Create', to develop insight about challenging and complex situations as seen in Table 2.2 below.

The process of deconstructing and reconstructing a situation involves connecting theory and social work practice through a process of critical reflection. In working alongside experienced social workers, discussions of child sexual abuse have exposed power dynamics which both underpin and restrict social work practice. This has taken place alongside a reworking of the presenting experience in a new and transformative way.

Other ways to use the tool

The **CSA Higher Order Thinking** tool can be used between a practice educator or on-site supervisor and learner to remind us that learning is an active process and can be applied in a structured way. The tool's principles also encourage learners to apply what they have learned to new contexts and situations, creating a transferable skill.

Table 2.2 CSA Higher Order Thinking tool

Level	Level	Action	3 questions/tasks
1	Remember	• Describe • Identify	1 Provide a concrete description of the situation as fully and detailed as I can (in written form and from my perspective). 2 Identify areas of risk and protective factors. 3 Describe the indicators of potential child sexual abuse and other overlapping categories of abuse.
2	Understand	• Explain • Summarise	1 In less than 3 minutes, accurately verbally summarise the key points of the situation, including any areas of concern. 2 Present my feelings about the circumstances. 3 Draw together the main threads of ideas about the presenting situation.
3	Apply	• Implement • Demonstrate	1 What theoretical perspective(s) helps make sense of this situation? Explain it through this lens. 2 How does my experience of this situation compare with previous or other experiences? 3 Draw a storymap (diagram of actors, events, issues) of the presenting situation.
4	Analyse	• Deconstruct • Break down	1 How might the situation be interpreted differently? For example, from the lived experience individual's perspective or from a different theoretical lens. 2 What patterns emerge from the description (Level 1)? 3 Consider any power dynamics which operate within the situation.

(Continued)

Table 2.2 *(Continued)*

Level	Level	Action	3 questions/tasks
5	Evaluate	• Critique • Argue (for/against)	1 Critically examine and weigh up the presenting information to assert my position and form a judgement about the situation. 2 Critique the possible underlying assumptions, interventions and solutions. 3 What research supports or challenges my understanding?
6	Create	• Generate • Reconstruct	1 Reconstruct the situation in light of the discussion expressed in supervision. 2 Does anything about my assumptions, theories or interpretations need to change? 3 Create new ways of seeing and understanding the situation.

Three key points

1 Remember social work's legal threshold for social work intervention is the 'balance of probabilities', so more than 50/50. On balance, should you intervene and is there anything you can do to make the child safer?

2 Remember the three important components for children when talking to someone about sexual abuse are 1. A sense of being believed, 2. Action is taken and 3. Emotional support is provided.

3 To deepen understanding of a situation involving CSA, it can be useful to engage in a deconstructive-reconstructive process of learning.

REFERENCES

Baldwin, C. (2013) *Narrative social work, theory and application*. Bristol: Policy Press.

Brookfield, S. (1997) *Developing critical thinking*. Buckinghamshire: The Open University Press.

CSA Centre (2022) *Training on intra-familial child sexual abuse for social work students – two approaches*. Available via: https://www.csacentre.org.uk/app/uploads/2023/10/Two_approaches_to_training_for_social_work_students_-_learning_report_Jan_2022.pdf

Glinski, A. (2019) *The myth of 'absolute knowing': when is the evidence enough?* Available via: https://www.csacentre.org.uk/blog/the-myth-of-absolute-knowing/

Glinski, A. and Sabin, N. (2022) *Communicating with children, A guide for those working with children who have or may have been sexually abused*. Available via: https://www.csacentre.org.uk/research-resources/practice-resources/communicating-with-children/

HM Government (2023) *Working together to safeguard children: A guide to inter-agency working to safeguard and promote the welfare of children*. London: DfE.

Hodger, H., Hurcombe, R., Redmond, T. and George, R. (2020) *"People don't talk about it": child sexual abuse in ethnic minority communities*. Available via: https://www.iicsa.org.uk/document/%E2%80%9Cpeople-dont-talk-about-it%E2%80%9D-child-sexual-abuse-ethnic-minority-communities

Howells (2023) 'Restorying trauma: Child sexual abuse', in Vine, T. and Richards, S. (eds.) *Stories, storytellers, and storytelling*. Cham, Switzerland: Palgrave Macmillan.

Karsna, K. and Bromley, P. (2024) *Child sexual abuse in 2022/23: trends in official data*. Available via: https://www.csacentre.org.uk/app/uploads/2024/02/Trends-in-Offical-Data-2022-23-FINAL.pdf

Karsna, K. and Kelly, L. (2021) *The scale and nature of child sexual abuse: Review of evidence*. Revised edn. Barkingside: CSA Centre..

Munro, E. (2011) *The Munro review of child protection. Final report. A child centred system*. London: The Stationery Office.

NPCC (2022) *National analysis of police-recorded child sexual abuse & exploitation (CSAE) Crimes report*. Available via: https://www.vkpp.org.uk/vkpp-work/analytical-capability/national-analysis-of-police-recorded-child-sexual-abuse-and-exploitation-crimes-report-2022/

Ormell, C.P. (1974) 'Bloom's taxonomy and the objectives of education', *Educational Research*, 17(1), pp. 3–18. doi:10.1080/0013188740170101.

Riessman, C. and Quinney, L. (2005) 'Narrative in social work, a critical review', *Qualitative Social Work : QSW : Research and Practice*, 4(4), pp. 391–412. [Online].

Senzaki, S., Hackathorn, J., Appleby, D.C. and Gurung, R.A.R. (2017) 'Reinventing flashcards to increase student learning', *Psychology Learning and Teaching*, 16(3), pp. 353–368. [Online].

Squire, C., Andrews, M. and Tamboukou, M. (2013) 'Introduction: What is narrative research?', in Andrews, M., Squire, C. and Tamboukou, M. (eds) *Doing narrative research*. 2nd edn. London: SAGE.

Vera-Gray, F. (2023) *Key messages from research of the impacts of child sexual abuse*. Available via: https://www.csacentre.org.uk/app/uploads/2023/03/Key-messages-from-research-Impacts-of-child-sexual-abuse.pdf

Chapter 3

Creating a welcome space in the margin of error: Finding a place for mistakes in social work

Rosslyn Dray

INTRODUCTION

Social work is a human and relationship-based practice (Dix et al., 2019) which inevitably has an interface with the possibility of mistakes. Rather than being something to wholly avoid, mistakes can create valuable learning opportunities for individuals, teams and organisations if the learning is harnessed (Schoemaker, 2011; Sicora, 2017a. Yet creating a welcome space for the possibility of making mistakes feels challenging. It is akin to asking a spider-phobic person to tolerate being in a room with a hairy tarantula.

Welcoming mistakes is not an ethos many social work practitioners or organisations feel comfortable to inhabit, especially when the impact of actions or inactions can have consequences for people's lives and choices. In social work, this is particularly pertinent if we encounter tragic outcomes such as the death of a child or adult at risk, or a situation where some form of harm occurs. This is a heavy emotional burden and one which influences the way we may make decisions or work with risk subsequently (Bryans, 1999; Reason, 1990; Sicora, 2017a, 2017b; Sicora et al., 2021). We are human and want to avoid doing harm.

Yet, mistakes can provide a gateway to opportunity and innovation as

> *diverse thinking and tolerance for mistakes are both critical to innovation since they allow for variation beyond what is normally seen.*
>
> (Schoemaker, 2011, pg. 7)

Whilst some mistakes can lead to harmful consequences and are desirable to avoid, there is also capital to gain from mistakes, as long as we commit to a

DOI: 10.4324/9781041054740-4

process of learning from them. Sicora (2017a, 2019) firmly places the process of reflection in working towards understanding and using mistakes as a means of learning. However, it requires the ability to sit with, tolerate and accept mistakes as an inevitable part of practice. This is something we sometimes need support to explore, and supervision is an excellent space for this.

WHAT IS A MISTAKE?

It is important to define what is a mistake before moving into the tools themselves. 'Mistake' is an English word derived from several source languages. The prefix of 'mis' originates from Old English and was used to mean 'bad' or 'badly' (Sedgwick, 2009). Further, a closely related Old Norse word 'mistaka' means to 'take in error' or 'miscarry' (Ayto, 2005). As spoken and written language has evolved, so to have use of words and meanings. They become an unquestioned part of social culture and communication. Interestingly, there is a close association of the verb to 'err' with error deriving from the Latin 'errare,' figuratively meaning to go astray (Ayto, 2005). Where mistakes are associated with error, or going wrong, it is unsurprising they are not seen as desirable.

Social work is an international profession, and it is interesting to see how 'mistake' is represented in various languages. There are words (Figure 3.1) which may appear similar to the English word 'mistake' which suggest a relationship between mistakes and negative connotations, for example, in Danish the word for mistake is 'fejl.'

James Reason (1990) wrote about organisational responses to error and differentiates how we understand types of error. Whilst there is not space to explore this fully, the context is helpful. Reason (1990) breaks down mistakes

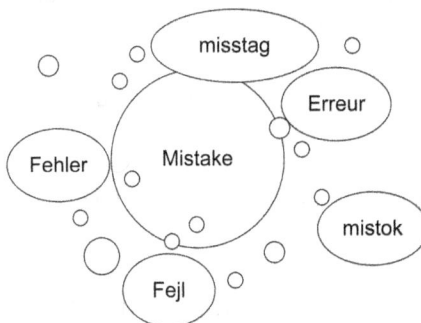

Figure 3.1 The word 'mistake' across languages

to look at intention and planning, arguing we need to understand the nature of the error and the factors which underly it. This goes beyond individual fault. For example, Reason differentiates between a trip, slip, lapse, lack of expertise or something which could have been prevented within wider systems (1990).

Importantly, Reason (1990) identifies the potential for error in systems and likens this to Swiss cheese. This metaphor visually suggests that there are holes in systems where latent errors can lurk, waiting for a trigger in the environment which can lead to a potential chain of consequence where the mistake is magnified. This perspective widens the scope of responsibility to a systemic lens enabling a broader evaluation of the situation. This is important because studies around mistakes show that individuals tend to assume disproportionate responsibility and emotional consequence, and this can skew effective evaluation of a situation (Bryans, 1999; Sicora, 2017, 2019). Further, Dekker (2014) states labelling something as a mistake is a retrospective action. It therefore suggests whether an event (intended or not) is a mistake is a question of individual judgement. It invites the question why it is labelled as such and who perceives it this way.

The potential for mistakes in social work is a reality. We work in a human profession where circumstances, resources and risks are dynamic, and other factors can influence outcomes. Participants in my research told me about their 'mistakes' which included, forgetting to record something they later realised was important, emailing the wrong recipient, completing paperwork incorrectly, making mistakes in financial calculations or doing something for the first time and not realising the correct procedure due to lack of experience and knowledge. As Schoemaker (2011) suggests, we may not also have all the information we need available to us at the point a decision or action is required. The tools which follow try to introduce some creativity, humour and ways of creating safer spaces to reflect whether that be in one-to-one supervision, or in teams.

Firstly, this chapter seeks to create spaces to re-examine our relationship with mistakes as the journey of learning starts from within. We will consider thoughts and feelings associated with this, and the risk involved in learning or trying something new. We will also look at ways we can foster more tolerant working cultures which recognise mistakes can create valuable learning opportunities, utilise diverse ideas and spark creativity. Who wouldn't want to be part of a more compassionate and reflexive social work profession? I hope you enjoy exploring these and thinking of ways you can use these in your practice or create your own!

DROPPING THE PEBBLE IN THE POND – USING IMMEDIATE ASSOCIATIONS TOOL

Figure 3.2 Dropping the pebble in the pond – using Immediate Associations tool

Inspiration

Part of my research has been to ask students and Practice Educators what they think of when they picture the word 'mistake.' I am curious how strong images come to mind, and one Practice Educator's description of a 'ripple effect' related to a time when she sent an email to the wrong person by mistake. A simple mistake, but she talked about the slooowww-motion realisation when she hit 'send,' the pit of stomach feeling, the frantic attempt to recall the message and then knowing the ripple of communication continued outside of her control. In the moment, I felt it with her and it made me think of ripples across a pond. I wondered about a tool which captured this as a way of reflecting.

Introduction

The **Dropping the pebble in the pond tool** (Figure 3.2) is presented in two ways, either as a mind map (version 1), or as a guided imagery exercise (version 2). It is a tool for any practitioner as it prompts self-reflection in an area often avoided, but one which is crucial to understanding how we may think, feel or behave in situations where mistakes may occur. It examines our relationship with mistakes; how we think and feel in the moment about mistakes, and how we connect those feelings to experiences where the ripple of consequence is felt. The tool has a specific purpose of connecting past feelings and experience with the present so practitioners can examine what has shaped their approach to mistakes and the impact this has on them as practitioners. It can be used individually but works best in a supervision session when you are guiding someone to reflect.

Theory

This tool is based on the technique of Free Association which finds its roots in psychoanalytic practice originating with the work of Freud (Craib, 2001). Psychosocial approaches foster the skill of reflexivity which creates a depth in our understanding of relationship dynamics in social work practice. It examines self in relation to others. It is sometimes easy for our thinking to become linear and rigid, or we may omit to look at the emotional 'baggage' we may be carrying into a situation.

The technique of Free Association (Hollway and Jefferson, 2000) can be useful in unlocking thinking and circumventing filters which may prevent us viewing a situation from other perspectives or indeed recognise where unconscious bias may influence thinking. The technique of Free Association is simply about getting the person to think of the immediate thoughts, feelings or experiences which come to mind in relation to a particular word, topic or experience. This technique is used within qualitative psychosocial research and therapeutic psychological settings to enable someone to access thoughts and feelings that have

> the kind of narrative that is not structured according to conscious logic....that is the associations follow pathways defined by emotional motivations, rather than rational intentions.
>
> (Hollway and Jefferson, 2000, pg. 37)

This may feel exposing and provide unanticipated insight, so it is important to create a safe space for the person to use this tool, for example, one-to-one supervision.

PAUSE TO REFLECT...

How can I create a safe and productive learning environment in supervision?

How to use the tool

This tool is presented in two ways. The first version is a mind map (Figure 3.3) below. You can simply use a blank sheet of paper and get the person to write the word 'mistake' in the middle, or if you are clever with graphics, you could create a template of your own to use!

Mind map – Blank template example – Version 1

Figure 3.4 below shows a mind map I created to look at my relationship with mistakes. As a researcher and practitioner, it was only fair I posed the same questions to myself, and it depicts my relationship with mistakes and where the ripples of past experience resonate for me in my practice. I am sharing this to show how it can be used as a springboard for reflection with words, pictures or whatever form of expression the individual wishes to use. I am no artist so using pictures from online worked well.

My relationship to mistakes – my mind map

You need a good open question to start off the reflection, for example,

> *Tell me about the thoughts, feelings and experiences in your mindmap that depict how you feel about mistakes.*

In asking curious questions, we need to be aware that sometimes the mistake feels big to the person. The metaphorical 'splash' of the pebble dropping creates

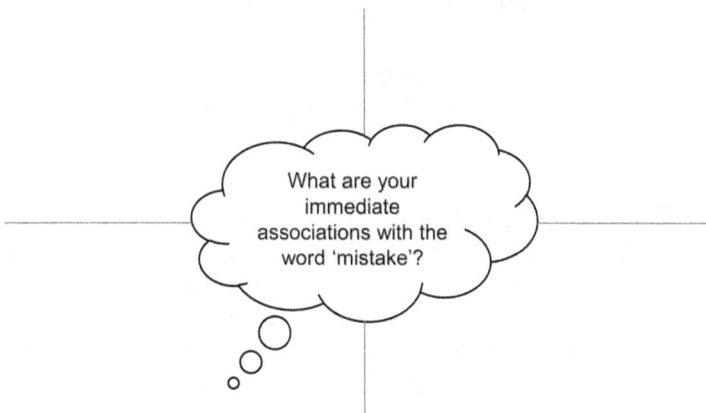

Figure 3.3 Mind map – blank template example – version 1

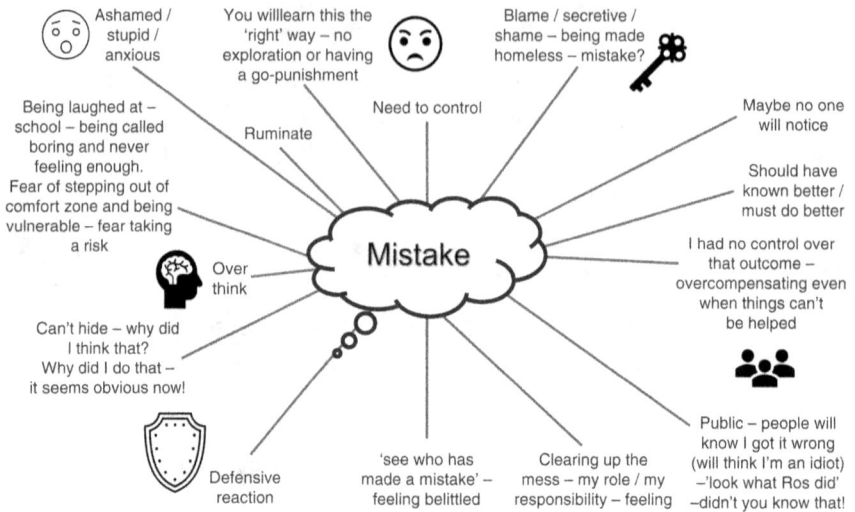

Figure 3.4 My relationship to mistakes – my mind map

waves across their emotions, perhaps distorting the reality of the impact of the mistake. It is about unpicking this with a sense of curiosity and sensitivity. In working with sensitive research topics, Hollway and Jefferson (2000) say the questions we ask are crucial. The 'why' questions, for example, may move a person towards intellectualising or justifying decisions, creating defensive responses (Hollway and Jefferson 2000). In evaluating a mistake, it may work better to use questions such as

> tell me about what happened or
> help me understand what you were feeling at that point or
> what changes were you aware of in your body at that time.

In essence, you are engaging with the person like you are a fellow traveller and validating that you too are a fallible human being (Gabriel and Ulus in Flam and Kleres ed, 2015).

The second version of the tool (Figure 3.4) uses guided imagery to prompt thoughts, feelings and experiences. Whichever method you choose, a quiet and private space is needed as you are asking someone to explore and reflect on personal experience. The guided story may suit someone who enjoys mindfulness practice or who would better engage with a guided story. You could, of course, use an actual pebble, writing 'mistake' on it in pen, and dropping it into a bowl of water so they can physically engage in the process of reflecting on their associations with the word mistake.

Just like the pebble, as individuals, we are invariably dropped into different environments. Paying attention to ourselves in relation to the wider environment can help us make sense of mistakes or actions and evaluate these in a more neutral way without over-valuing what we did 'wrong.' The ripple effect of this is something which enables us to understand and calibrate our actions. The imagery is a gentle way of engaging with a different type of thinking, where we abstract ourselves from the present and bring focus by transporting our imagination to a calm place. This is a technique often used in mindfulness practice, but it is a useful skill to develop in terms of being able to tune into our thoughts and feelings, where they come from, and what influence they have on how we think and feel in the present.

DROPPING THE PEBBLE IN THE POND – GUIDED STORY

Imagine a place where you are sat on the edge of a stream. This place is somewhere you feel relaxed, and calm and safe. You have no distractions.

There is a small pool of clear water, and you are looking into it. You see a pebble on the ground, and you pick it up. You are holding the pebble in your hand. You can sense it and you turn to look at it. You notice it's shape, it's texture and the feel against your skin....

You also notice it has the word mistake written on it in your handwriting. This pebble represents your relationship to mistakes.

In your own time, you drop the pebble into the clear water below. You observe the noise it makes as you drop it into the water, and watch it sink slowly to the bottom. You hold your pebble in sight, but you move your attention slowly as you notice it has disturbed the surface of the water....

On the surface of the water, you observe a series of ripples gently emanating from where the pebble entered. These represent your thoughts and feelings about mistakes that the pebble has contained. Your move your awareness to these thoughts and feelings....

You notice them … as each one comes to mind. They are thoughts. They are feelings. You may notice feelings in your body as those thoughts surface.

You notice you attach words to them, and these words remind you of experiences as the ripple travels across the surface of the water. You bring each one gently into your awareness and watch as each one then drifts across the water.

Figure 3.5 Pebbles

After some time, the ripples subside and the water becomes still. Your pebble is at the bottom of the pool (Figure 3.5). You observe the word mistake lifting from the surface of the pebble and dissolving into the water.

You bring your attention back to the present in your own time. Re-focus and notice your surroundings.

In your own time, either write down or share some of the thoughts, feelings or experiences which came to mind.

Other ways to use the tool

This tool can be used in various ways so you can let your imagination run free. A Practice Educator, On-site supervisor and learner could use this tool in supervision at different stages through the placement, e.g. as part of induction and getting to know each other in supervision, or if a mistake occurs. Alternatively, the tool could be used alongside someone with lived experience if you are doing reflective work on barriers to change where there is fear in trying new experiences or learning new things.

Conclusion

This part has been introspective and about examining and exploring our relationship to mistakes. The purpose of understanding this is to make sense of how we operate and increase our professional self-awareness. When we are conscious of something and it is in our awareness, we can do something about it. It is the foundation of reflexive practice.

THE FIRST ATTEMPTS IN LEARNING (F.A.I.L) TOOL

Figure 3.6 The First Attempts in Learning (F.A.I.L.) tool

Inspiration

I was talking with a colleague, and she said her daughter had just had a 'FAIL' (first attempt in learning) week at school. I thought this was a clever idea to help students normalise how mistakes are a part of learning and that anticipating mistakes gives people permission to have a go. I thought it would be good to use this in my role working with social work students and I thought it would also be a great experiential tool for Practice Educators and On-site Supervisors to show how we should anticipate mistakes as part of the process of learning ... and so the **'FAIL' tool** *was born.*

Introduction

The **F.A.I.L. tool** (Figure 3.6) is about remembering how it feels to learn something new for the first time. It is about exploring how we feel when there is a risk of mistakes, and what support we may need to tolerate that uncertainty. The point of this is to normalise mistakes, raise self-awareness, manage uncertainty and seek to learn and reflect from experience.

The tool looks at how we plan, carry out and evaluate tasks, the support we seek (or not) and the impact this has. This is also about promoting conversations about reflection and self-awareness. The tool itself is something you would use and then invite reflective conversations about the process that happened. It is something which works best in a group or team setting as it shows how people approach tasks in different ways to achieve the same outcome. This tool is something I have used in a group teaching session with Practice Educators and On-site Supervisors in getting them to reflect how it feels to be a learner, and also how it feels to support someone learning.

There are two stages to this tool, the 'doing' stage and the 'reflection' stage. Each is led by the group facilitator. Drawing is not a natural comfort zone for many people, so this has given opportunities to reflect on how we respond when put under pressure to complete a task we are unfamiliar with. It is important to create a safe learning environment and to give permission for people to complete the task in whatever way they feel will work. This has worked well in group settings and generated a lot of humour which has been a useful tool to discuss the learning afterwards.

This tool highlights the many different ways one can approach a task. Encouraging different approaches means we experience the benefits of diverse thinking strategies, and this can support innovation, celebrate neurodiversity, and creativity in teams. It also helps us learn from the process when things don't go quite to plan or we F.A.I.L.

Theory

Experiential learning is an approach to learning which places experience and reflection at the centre of activity. Kolb's (1984) cycle of learning around experience enables practitioners to work through stages of reflection, analysis, evaluation and action. Other learning theorists have developed these ideas, acknowledging the multi-sensory nature of learning which Kolb's model does not reflect (Mietinnen, 2010). Peter Jarvis (2010) talks about the sensory and lifelong nature of learning, and how significant moments, such as making a mistake, can create opportunities to reflect and develop new understanding.

Concepts of growth and fixed mindsets relate to how we feel about mistakes and are based on the work of Carol Dweck around the characteristics of learners (2000, 2019). Her research mainly focused on children in education, but the concepts transpose to how this impacts our approach to learning as adults. It is possible to move between a fixed or growth mindset and it is good to be aware of the impact of this on our ability to reflect and evaluate. The text box outlines the key differences between a person with a fixed or growth mindset. This helps us understand why a learner may find it difficult to accept feedback or process mistakes, and helps us identify ways to work with the learner to overcome this.

How to use the tool

Characteristics of a 'fixed mindset'

- There is only one way to do things – right or wrong.
- Intelligence and ability are fixed traits – cannot be improved/changed.
- Person-focused feedback – engenders criticism and creates defensiveness. It focuses on the outcome only and feels personal e.g. *'you did this, and this happened.'*
- Possibility of failure is not tolerated and therefore discourages exploration and option seeking.

Characteristics of a 'growth mindset'

- Understanding there are often multiple approaches or ways of doing things.
- Process-focused feedback – focusing on the strategy adopted and not the outcome – feedback that is effort and ability orientated – how the person has approached it and evaluating the effort they put into forming the strategy e.g. 'I can understand why you may have approached it this way…'
- Questioning – what can you learn from this experience?
- Recognising mistakes, failure or setbacks is an expected part of learning.

(adapted from Haimovitz and Dweck, 2017)

The tool itself is a set of instructions for the facilitator, some paper, pens and a selection of images (like the ones printed in Figure 3.7a, b and c below) or of your own choosing from which participants complete the task. When using in a group, typically it takes time to organise people into pairs and get participants to take a risk and work with someone they may not usually work with!

Figure 3.7 Illustrations: (a) butterfly, (b) elephant, (c) lion

This tool does require the responsiveness of the facilitator to ask questions and prompt reflections from the participants after the exercise in completed. The reflection stage is where interesting insights emerge and are shared! This always creates useful insights into how people approach a new task, the solutions they create, or what support they look for/or want to provide. Importantly, it can show us how we feel where there is risk around the unfamiliar, or potential for mistakes.

The key to delivering this tool is giving simple directions and not giving any leading direction on how to complete the task. It is good for participants to feel a little uncertainty to simulate how it feels to do something for the first time, and where there is the possibility of mistakes.

Things you need:

- Pencil or pen
- Blank paper
- Table/desk to work on
- Pictures from which to copy.
  Tip: I tend to select two to three different pictures which can be spread across the group. I have provided examples of the ones I use but you can choose your own! The key to this is picking something which requires some skill, but not the artistic ability of Leonardo De Vinci.
- Sense of humour and willingness to have a go.

F.A.I.L. TOOL FACILITATOR INSTRUCTIONS:

1 You will need to work in pairs.
2 One person is going to be the person who is going to do a task they have not done before (learner). One person is going to be the person who is supporting them in undertaking this new task (their supervisor). Decide who you are going to be and find a space to work.

(Facilitator gives out pictures FACE DOWN so participants do not know what the task is going to be. Provide blank paper and pen/pencil.)

3   Facilitator says to participants:

Your task is to make a copy of the image on the blank paper you have been given. You have 5 minutes to complete the task, but you need to first discuss and agree a plan with your supervisor on how you plan to approach the task (7 minutes in total).

4   Say '**turn over the paper and begin.**'

N.B the instructions are deliberately vague to encourage people to choose how they will complete the task. Some participants will find this strange and may seek guidance. Keep the instruction as above. Any hesitation or seeking certainty in concrete instructions can be explored in the reflection afterwards.

As facilitator make sure you observe the group. This is your chance to note anything which stands out, and any moments where there are things you pick up on which can be used in the reflection afterwards. I tend to find there is nervous laughter, or people trying different ways to complete the task, such a tracing and then perceiving this to be 'cheating.' There is always something interesting to reflect on and no 'right' or 'wrong' approach to take.

Reflection stage:

Once the task is completed, the facilitator will lead reflection on the activity. You are trying to explore how it felt for participants to approach a new task, and how it felt to try and support someone doing something new. You can either do the reflection as a whole group, or you can start by inviting the pairs to reflect with each other, and then contribute feedback on their experiences to the wider group.

Here are some reflective questions to use (feel free to add your own!)

1   What were your immediate feelings about being asked to do this?
2   On a scale of 1–10 how far were you out of your comfort zone (1 = totally out of comfort zone/10 = completely comfortable) – both partners in the pair.
3   In what way did this influence how you approached the task, or supporting the learner.

4   Did this change as the task went on? What feelings or thoughts were you aware of?
5   What did your partner observe? (e.g. body language, words, actions)
6   How did it feel to have limited instructions on how to approach the task?
7   What options did you consider in approaching the task and what influence did the view of your partner have?
8   What influence did other people's approach have on how you undertook this?
9   How involved were you in supporting once the task was underway? How did this feel? Any reflections?
10   How was feedback, guidance or encouragement given and received?

Additional questions:

1   What have I learnt about myself or from this experience?
2   What have I learnt about how I support others from this experience?
3   How will my practice benefit from this awareness?
4   What are the areas of development I need to work on?

Other ways to use the tool

This tool is something which can be used in practice learning. I have used it many times with training Practice Educators and On-site Supervisors to help them remember what it feels like to learn something new, and what approaches we take to support learners. It always creates humour and rich reflection.

The principle of 'F.A.I.L' is something which could also be incorporated into supervision discussions by adding it to the supervision agenda to both reflect on moments of success, and moments where there has been a 'F.A.I.L.' This ensures these moments are discussed, and the learning drawn from them in a non-stigmatised way.

Conclusion

Where people are in a zone of play or creativity (promoting oxytocin) rather than a testosterone-driven environment it can positively switch the energy of a group and stimulate good reflection. It is important to establish cultures in teams where mistakes are acknowledged to be part of our ongoing learning. If we trigger blame or shame, it can promote a culture where mistakes are concealed and avoided (Sicora in Frost eds 2018). If practitioners can be open when things do not quite go to plan, it creates more ethically sound practice and a culture where we can productively learn from unanticipated outcomes.

Remember, the 'blooper reel' in a film is often the funniest and most unguarded moments of the production. Sometimes it is more entertaining than the film itself. Whilst we don't seek to make 'bloopers' or mistakes, they can and will happen at times, and we need to recognise this is part of being human. Using humour softens the experience and acknowledges that humanity. Creating honesty and candour around our mistakes is important.

THE 'MY MISTAKE?' TOOL

Self-reflection	Me	My thoughts at the time	My feelings at the time	My thoughts and feelings now?
Reflection and analysis of self and wider factors	Wider factors	What was going on in the environment? Were there slip hazards I didn't anticipate?	• Organisational factors? • Team atmosphere / pressures? • Relationships? • Resource constraints or considerations?	Learning this highlights for team or organisation ⬛ Service or process errors or gaps?
Learning Evaluate options, learning and action	Learning this highlights for me? With hindsight what would I do differently? Points where I may have made a different decision? Slip or trip hazards my actions / decisions influenced through lack of knowledge?	What were the other available and realistic options open to me to consider? Would this have been in my control or not?	How would I plan things differently if I were to encounter something similar?	Gaps in my tool kit or knowledge I have become aware of? How can I address it and what support might I need?

Figure 3.8 The 'my mistake?' tool

Inspiration

I am the first person to over-value my role in a mistake and dwell on the uncomfortable feelings it creates. My research participants also consistently talked about similar reactions but crucially described the process of 'stepping back.' This is something we have to purposefully do to evaluate a situation and get to a place of being able to see the bigger picture. So, I created this grid to help think *about all the other things which could be part and parcel of a mistake in terms of environmental and systemic factors to help my students when they make mistakes in their practice learning. I called it '***my mistake?***' as I want this to be about seeing mistakes in a context and being able to evaluate them usefully.*

Introduction

The '**my mistake?**' **tool** (Figure 3.8) is a way of enabling someone to think outside of themselves and their role in a mistake so they can evaluate and learn from a situation.

The tool is a pictorial grid which could be printed off for supervision as a discussion prompt around the analysis and evaluation of an unwanted or unintended outcome. The aim is to provide both a focused (deep dive) reflection and to create a more landscape opportunity to view risk and factors which affected the decision or outcome.

Theory

The elements of this tool are based on the work of James Reason (1990) in relation to error and differentiating the different types or mistake and causes. This leads to wider evaluation of factors influencing mistakes which are sometimes outside of our control. Reason (1990) uses the metaphor of Swiss Cheese (Figure 3.9) to describe how errors can sit latently within systems whereby some action or inaction triggers a chain of consequence.

Research into professional mistakes and mistakes in social work (Bryans, 1999; Sicora, 2017a, 2017b, 2019) highlights the strong presence of emotion in the process of evaluation and how this can draw our perspective too heavily on our personal role in a mistake or unintended/unwanted outcome. This can hamper the evaluation process for the individual, leading to avoidance of the issue or defensive reasoning (Tavris and Aronson, 2020). Supervision is a space where we can explore and try to model adaptive responses which reduce shame in the individual by considering the context deliberately (Sicora in Frost eds 2018).

Figure 3.9 Cheese

How to use the tool

The grid is something which can be used within a supervision conversation. It can be used as a prompt to allow for analysis and evaluation through questions which guide the conversation. You would start by looking at the top left of the grid (the 'my' part in the mistake). This part asks the person reflecting to think about feelings then and now. Sometimes we can acknowledge the fading intensity of our emotional response as the distance between the consequence and impact increases, we can then use hindsight to recognise and learn from how that may have impacted our decision-making or actions at the time, and how it may feel now. Moreover, what you may change as a result of that knowledge. The tool then guides you to broaden the conversation out to look at the wider environmental and systemic factors (outlined in the boxes across it) and the learning which can be drawn from the experience.

Using open questions prompt the reflector to explore – you want them to take you on their journey. Here are a few example questions…

Tell me what was going on for you at the time or
Describe for me how you felt that day or
Talk me through how you decided to approach that task.

The approach of this tool is exploratory. To begin using the tool you could suggest your supervisee brings a case outcome to reflect on which has had challenges, unintended or perhaps unwanted consequences. Sometimes amidst challenge, positive outcomes can become hidden, so it is also an opportunity to see if any discoveries or unexpected (good!) outcomes have come about, for example, a mistake may expose a learning need.

Example

In using this, I have incorporated pictures, for example, the banana skin. It helps students understand the nature of the mistake they are reflecting on, e.g. was this a slip (the banana skin) or something which came about through a lack of planning or resource. It is really important to get them to think about why the mistake may have happened in a blame-free way. Sometimes it highlights a lack of skills in an area. This links back to the theory behind it, because if we are not aware of something, or have yet to learn it, do we label it a 'mistake' or is it an opportunity that has presented itself to highlight an area of learning? This gives me the opportunity to question this with my students.

I also wanted to include reflection on feelings as some students I have worked with feel less able to articulate feelings, fearing being seen as 'unprofessional' if they have an emotional reaction. They quickly move into what they thought. Pausing to consider feelings is what comes before thought and an important part of their sensory experience to process and understand.

Other ways to use the tool

This is a tool which can be adapted depending on the context the practitioner is working within, and who they are working with. I have used this in a teaching context asking students to evaluate a situation retrospectively where a mistake occurs, or where they are placing too much emphasis on their emotional reaction to a mistake and need to be encouraged to evaluate the situation in a more balanced way.

You could also adapt this idea to use with a person with lived experience around mistakes and in situations where they may need support to look at the wider picture and increase their awareness of factors outside of their control.

Alternatively, you could adapt it to use at different stages of an intervention if you are supporting a student or newly qualified worker to plan or evaluate their approach in a situation, e.g. anticipating risks or potential errors. It is presented as a retrospective thinking tool here but could easily be adapted.

Conclusion

It takes courage to own and reflect on situations where we wish the outcome was different. Often, we can focus too much on our responsibility or want to avoid looking at the issues because of our feelings towards the situation or outcome. This is where supervision and a guided conversation can help, and I hope this tool may be of use. If we take a broader perspective, we can highlight areas of learning not only for ourselves, but potentially in services or procedures, and it teaches us the skills of evaluation which add genuine value to service improvement.

Summary points:

1   **Re-evaluate what mistakes mean to you** and normalise them as part of a process of your continuous professional development. Do this for yourself and model this in your practice.

2   **Learning begins with making a commitment to reflect and the courage to examine ourselves**. Who we are in the present is a product of our experiences. To be effective in our practice, and to understand the impact of self on those we work with, we need to make a commitment to explore our relationship with mistakes.

3   **The use of creativity and humour can create a different energy within ourselves and teams.** As a profession, social work values creativity and resourcefulness and these only come about when we have the courage to try different things. Why not use play, creativity and humour to help foster a more productive learning environment?

Having a more balanced view of mistakes means we are more likely to learn from situations where outcomes are unexpected. If we make a welcome space for mistakes in social work practice, there is space to evaluate practice more realistically. It may also mean more willingness to examine and understand how things can be done differently when evaluation is not driven by the emotional impact of blame or shame. What may be viewed as a mistake may lead to discovering new ways of working or innovation, as there have been some great inventions which were in fact, mistakes … chocolate chip cookie anyone?

REFERENCES

Ayto, J. (2005) *Word origins. The origins of thousands of words in the English language explored and explained*. 2nd edn. London: A & C Black.

Bryans, P. (1999) 'What do professional men and women learn from making mistakes at work?', *Research in Post Compulsory Education*, 4(2), pp. 183–194.

Craib, I. (2001) *Psychoanalysis: A critical introduction*. Cambridge, UK: Polity Press.

Dekker, S. (2014) *The field guide to understanding human error*. 3rd edn. Florida: CRC press.

Dix, H., Hollinrake, S. and Meade, J.(eds.) (2019) *Relationship-based social work with adults*. St Albans: Critical Publishing Ltd.

Dweck, C.S. (2000) *Self theories; Their role in motviation, personality and development*. London: Psychology Press.

Dweck, C.S. (2019) The choice to make a difference. *Perspectives on Psychological Science*, 14(1), pp. 21–25.

Flam, H. and Kleres, J.(eds.) (2015) *Methods of exploring emotions*. London: Routledge.

Frost, L., Magyar-Haas, V., Schoneville, H. and Sicora, A. (eds.) (2018) *Shame and social work, theory, reflexivity and practice*. Bristol: Policy Press.

Haimovitz, K. and Dweck, C.S. (2017) 'The origins of children's growth and fixed mindsets: New research and a new proposal', *Child Development*, (online) 88(6), pp. 1849–1859.

Hollway, W. and Jefferson, T. (2000) *Doing qualitative research differently - free association, narrative and the interview method*. London: Sage.

Jarvis, P. (2010) *Adult education and lifelong learning: Theory and practice*. 4th edn. London: Routledge.

Kolb, D.A. (1984) *Experiential learning*. Englewood Cliffs, NJ: Prentice Hall.

Mietinnen, R. (2010) *The concept of experiential learning and John Dewey's theory of reflective thought and action*.

Reason, J. (1990) *Human error*. Cambridge: Cambridge University Press.

Schoemaker, P.J.H. (2011) *Brilliant mistakes*. Philadelphia: Wharton Digital Press.

Sedgwick, F. (2009) *Where words come from – A dictionary of word origins*. London: Continuum International Publishing Group.

Sicora, A. (2017a) *Reflective practice and learning from mistakes in social work*. Bristol: Policy Press.

Sicora, A. (2017b) 'Reflective practice, risk and mistakes in social work', *Journal of Social Work Practice*, 31(4), pp. 491–502.

Sicora, A. (2019) 'Reflective practice and learning from mistakes in social work student placement', *Social Work Education*, 38(1), pp. 63–67.

Sicora, A., Lu, W. and Lei, J. (2021) 'Exploring mistakes and errors of professional judgement in social work in China and Italy: The impact of culture organisation and education', *Journal of Social Work*, 21(5), pp. 1065–1083.

Tavris, C. and Aronson, E. (2020) *Mistakes were made but not by me*. London: Pinter and Martin.

Chapter 4

Creatively applying professional dangerousness to improve practice responses to risk situations

Nora Duckett

INTRODUCTION

Placing together 'professional' and 'dangerousness' may seem like a contradiction in terms. Where 'professional' is used as a noun to represent the desired and elevated qualities, knowledge and skills of qualified people in a specific discipline and 'dangerousness' as 'the quality or state of being likely to cause danger' (Merriam-Webster Dictionary, 2024), it is reasonable to question how they make sense together. In the context of safeguarding and protection social work, professional dangerousness can be understood as the dynamic interplay of organisational and social relationships where practitioners are making sense of and responding to concerns about the risk of abuse. Professional dangerousness as a concept offers a way of recognising and encouraging practitioners and managers to countenance the possibility whereby "... *protective intentions and actions can inadvertently be contributing to extending dangerous behaviour in some families*" (Calder, 2008, p. 61).

Professional dangerousness applies to practitioners from any discipline, and according to Calder (2008, p. 61), "*early recognition and identification of the concept promotes safe professional practice*". This chapter aims to revisit and reformulate the concept in a way that makes it accessible and applicable yet, at the same time, acknowledges social work is inherently complex (Hood, 2014) and that it is characterised by uncertainties and contingencies, and each child or adult and family's unique situation requires a personalised practice response. Another unequivocal assertion is that no single tool or approach can take the place of well-supported practitioners working together in well-resourced services and teams, agreeing and respectfully disagreeing and implementing robust, multi-agency plans, in accordance with statutory guidelines. Practitioners are generally knowledgeable and skilful at identifying risks and deciding on what needs to be done. Decisions are made collectively by groups of professionals, who focus on the individual's needs

DOI: 10.4324/9781041054740-5

by actively listening to the child or adult and their support networks, observing behaviours and contexts, and thoroughly examining, evaluating and applying relevant theoretical, research, legal and policy evidence. Although this chapter primarily focuses on social work with children and families, the concepts discussed can also be applied to understanding professional responses to adults at risk of abuse and neglect. Additionally, this chapter includes two interactive **checklists** designed to support understanding and recall and challenge assumptions and biases while proactively applying the concept of professional dangerousness.

PROFESSIONAL DANGEROUSNESS – A PRACTICE EXAMPLE

It wasn't until I'd been a social worker for over 10 years and a family support practitioner for 5 years that I first heard the term 'professional dangerousness'. It wasn't mentioned in my degree course or in subsequent course learning or by practice educators, supervisors, peers, or team managers. When I learnt about it, I felt both relief and regret – relief in understanding it and regret for not knowing it earlier in my career. I recognised moments where the concept applied, like when I hesitated to discuss a risky situation with a colleague I didn't trust or when I was intimidated by a family and relieved when they (appeared) not to be at home. I also realised there were times when I focused too much on empathising with adults and spent less time with the children or when I placed too much emphasis on material goods to resolve issues related to chronic neglect. Acknowledging mistakes is tough, but they remind me that even with the best intentions, I've made errors that could have led to poor outcomes. Since learning about professional dangerousness, I've worked to better understand it and share this knowledge with others.

What is professional dangerousness? – An introduction to the checklist

Types of professional dangerousness have been identified over time as learning has taken place from analysing the tragic events where a child or adult has been fatally or seriously harmed. The concept is useful in supporting critical reflection and reflexivity and as a means of analysing available information. Social workers use a range of methods to assess and manage risk, including using intuitive reasoning and analysis (Munro, 2007), and actuarial models based on scientific and statistical data (Taylor, 2017). Heuristic models are described as "any approach to judgement that simplifies information to manage complexity, regardless of the extent to which this has been studied (or not) within academic disciplines" (Taylor, 2017, p. 1046). Characteristics of professional dangerousness could then be considered a type of heuristic, or shorthand approach to supporting professional judgement and decision-making. The emphasis here is not about risk eradication, as this is not possible (Kemshall, 2013). It is about how risk is managed and how the concept can support critical reflection and professional curiosity (Duckett, 2022, in Dix and Howells, 2022) in making sense of the available information and (inter- and intra-) professional responses.

The following **checklist** (Table 4.1 adapted from Davies and Duckett, 2016, pp. 7–8), sets out 14 examples of professional dangerousness, describes their characteristics and includes research evidence. To support accessibility and understanding, each type or pattern of professional dangerousness is presented separately, as if they are static and standalone; however, they inevitably overlap as they attempt to describe the dynamic interplay of social, organisational and professional systems and responses to risk situations in families and within professional and organisational networks. Munro (2007, p. 52) advocates for the use of **checklists** (Figure 4.1) as one way of reminding professionals of factors to take into consideration and as a counterbalance to selective use of information.

PROFESSIONAL DANGEROUSNESS PATTERNS AND CHARACTERISTICS CHECKLIST

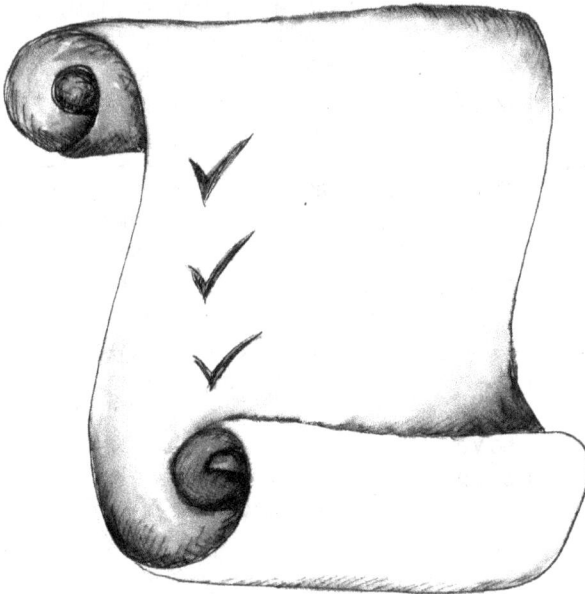

Figure 4.1 Professional dangerous patterns and characteristics checklist

Table 4.1 Professional dangerousness checklist

Children and carers unheard	Reviews into children's deaths and serious injuries consistently point to how children were not sufficiently listened to. Children can find it hard to talk about their experiences of abuse and research shows that despite trying to communicate what is happening to them and their feelings, they are not heard (Allnock and Miller, 2013; Office of the Children's Commissioner, 2015). Helm (2011) argues that practitioners must accept the reality of uncertainty and that not doing so affects how children's views are sought and regarded. As well, when parents and carers try to tell professionals that they are afraid they may hurt a child or that they cannot cope, this is not always acted on in a timely way (Reder and Duncan, 1995).
Rule of optimism	A rule of optimism attempts to describe organisational and professional tendencies to want to believe that all is well for the child (or adult), even where indicators of abuse may be available or visible. The term was coined by Dingwall, Eekelaar and Murray (1983) not to draw attention to or blame individual failings but to describe their observation of the systemic process whereby resource-strapped health and children's services filtered the large population of children in need from the smaller population defined as 'serious' and requiring recourse to the law. The concept is also associated with an unchecked 'natural love' assumption, which is a belief that parents naturally love their children and do not normally intend to harm them. Studies of serious case reviews (Brandon *et al.*, 2009) found that practitioners tended to accept or take at face value what they were told by parents and carers and did not effectively obtain children's perspectives.
Concrete solutions	This is dangerous practice when reactions to concerns about risk are purely or overly practical and sometimes rapid ways of responding to often deep-seated, emotionally based problems (Reder and Duncan, 1999). Providing washing machines, furniture, accommodation or finance, or, for instance, referring to parenting or anger management courses, without the accompanying questioning of underlying issues or assumptions and prejudicial factors affecting the family, adult or child. Clarity is required about how exactly each practical input will bring about the necessary change in a realistic timeframe to reduce or manage risk. Poverty has been described as 'the wallpaper of practice' (Morris *et al.*, 2018) to convey its normalisation by professionals, which may also deflect or obscure risk of harm indicators.

(Continued)

Table 4.1 *(Continued)*

Assessment paralysis	In this type of professional dangerousness, change is perceived as too hard or impossible to achieve because of beliefs within the professional network that the family has always been this way. Alongside this, excessive anxiety and feeling overwhelmed may lead to an inability to think and to professional inaction (Ferguson, 2018; Reder and Duncan, 1999; Reder, Duncan and Gray, 1993). Professionals may feel helpless, overwhelmed and incapacitated when tasked with assessment and investigation of risk. Chronic neglect is often normalised because of this approach.
Stereotyping and Cultural relativism	Assumptions are made about how families care for children (and adults), which include stereotypes and cultural relativism (Webb, Maddocks and Bongilli, 2002; Taylor et al., 2024). Bernard's (2019) research points to professionals' lack of detection of abuse in affluent families, which in part is attributed to professional biases based on status and class and adults'/carers' power to limit and shape assessment and investigation. The Independent Inquiry Child Sexual Abuse (IICSA) (2020) reported on how cultural stereotypes and racism lead to institutional and professional failure to identify and respond appropriately to child sexual abuse and make it more difficult for children and other individuals to talk about child sexual abuse. Adultification is a form of stereotyping of Black children from global majorities as being less in need of protection (Davies, 2022). Professionals operating cultural relativism in relation to Victoria Climbié justified indicators of abuse as cultural difference (Batty, 2002).
Closure and Avoidance	Within these types of professionally dangerous practices, families are seen to shut out professionals by not answering calls, missing appointments and not responding to home visits. Reder, Duncan and Gray (1993) found closure to be the most significant indicator of danger in family and professional interaction, as deaths from abuse are often preceded by closure. Closure may be mirrored by professionals avoiding contact with the family, and research (Brandon *et al.*, 2009; Littlechild, 2005, 2012) has found that professional responses to parental avoidance, violence and intimidation can result in worker avoidance, victimisation and fear of challenging abusive behaviour.

(Continued)

Table 4.1 *(Continued)*

Priority given to recent information	Information which is recent, emotional and vivid takes precedence over the old (Munro, 2007). Inquiries demonstrate that agencies held a great deal of knowledge and understanding about actual or potential harm to the child but did not give this due weight in their analysis (Brandon *et al.*, 2009). New information must be examined in the context of prior facts. The importance of chronologies to allow analysis cannot be overemphasised.
Non-compliance with statutory procedures	Inquiries commonly report that legislation, policy and practice are sound but that professionals did not comply with their implementation. When formal child protection procedures are in place, enabling collation and analysis of available information, children are generally well protected. Laming (2003, p. 4) stated his amazement that professionals in key agencies did not follow relatively straightforward procedures on how to respond where there is concern about significant harm.
Role confusion	Professionals may be unclear about safeguarding tasks and assume that someone else is responsible for undertaking them, leading to a lack of coordinated action. Assumptions like these are often noted in safeguarding practice and learning reviews and where practitioners take on the role and responsibilities of other workers or deny the relevance of their qualifications and statutory powers (Reder, Duncan and Gray, 1993). In safeguarding work everyone has responsibility for the safety of the child (or adult); however, clarity of roles, tasks and timeframes in decision-making is essential.
Exaggeration of hierarchy	People who may be considered to have low status who report abuse may not be taken seriously even though they may be close to the world of the child, e.g. neighbours, friends or a nursery worker. A psychiatrist, lawyer or paediatrician may be heard more readily or given more weight by professionals. White and Featherstone's (2005) research found social workers and health professionals referring to other professionals' failings in terms of recognising child abuse, which may indicate a process of accentuating their own professional expertise as somehow more than or outside of the professional team. Brandon *et al.*'s (2009) analysis of reviews into child deaths and serious injury in Wales indicated that a lack of respect or mistrust of other professionals' perspectives led to communication breakdown.

(Continued)

Table 4.1 *(Continued)*

Stockholm syndrome	This example is based on -situations where people taken hostage begin to identify with the captors' cause as a means of survival. This is a mechanism used in child sexual abuse (Julich, 2005). Sometimes a parent or carer who is abusive is powerful, intimidating and maybe critical of professionals, and the practitioner begins to identify with their point of view rather than the child's (or the at risk adult's). The worker may feel safe but at the expense of the child (or adult). Gender may well be a component, given most social workers are women who may feel intimidated and fear violence from male perpetrators. It can also be thought of as a 'trauma bonding'.
Omnipotence	Professionals may believe that their knowledge about and relationship with the family or individual is superior to others' and that they alone know what is in the best interests of the child or adult they are working with. Within this dynamic, professionals tend not to revisit their perceptions in the light of new evidence. Mason's (2022) 'unsafe certainty' can be viewed as a type of dangerousness whereby professionals' feelings of being stuck and desire for certainty leads to lack of creativity, and dogmatic and defensive practice.
False or disguised compliance	Parents and carers may try to convince professionals that they are cooperating to protect the child or adult, which is inauthentic. Professionals may then be persuaded of their cooperation and become enmeshed with the family and collusive with the parents/carers, which can obscure the child's (or adult's) needs (Littlechild, 2005; Reder and Duncan, 1999; Reder, Duncan and Gray, 1993).
Professional accommodation syndrome	The professional may mirror the child's retraction of abuse, deny the reality and be keen to be persuaded that any allegation by the child must be suppressed. Any other possible reason for the abuse will tend to become accepted in preference to considering the possibility that abuse has occurred (Morrison, 1990). This parallels Summit's (1983) child sexual abuse accommodation syndrome.

Source: Adapted from Davies and Duckett (2016, pp. 7–8).

Critique

While professional dangerousness provides a valuable lens for social work practice, it is subject to critique, particularly regarding power imbalances and intersectional, contextual and cultural factors. Calder (2008) argues that professional dangerousness should be understood within organisational contexts, viewing it systemically and not as a way of affording individual blame. This helps to see the influence of cultural and structural issues, such as chronic underfunding and high and unmanageable caseloads, on professional practice. Two frequently questioned concepts are a rule of optimism and disguised compliance. A rule of optimism, though frequently referred to in analyses of learning from where children have not been safeguarded (Dickens et al., 2002) s, has been misapplied to blame individual practitioners for failings and naivety (Kettle and Jackson, 2017). Dingwall (2013), one of its originators, has also criticised its use as part of hindsight bias instead of as an analytic tool. Disguised or false compliance has been described as misleading and as a flawed diagnostic tool that sets parents and carers up to fail (Leigh, Beddoe and Keddell, 2020). Clearly, if used uncritically and where parents or carers are responding through fear, or as a learnt or trauma response to power and authority, or through lack of understanding of what is required, it would be unethical and oppressive. It is essential to critically evaluate these constructs if they are to be helpful in reducing risk and consider the impact of social inequalities and cultural, political and relational dimensions of practice.

Underpinning theory

The concept of professional dangerousness first appears in Dingwall, Eekelaar and Murray's (1983) research, where the focus came to be on the process by which health and social services determined children in need of protection and potentially requiring legal intervention from those in general need. They found professional decision-making involved inferring the moral character of family members and opting for the least stigmatising interpretation of the available information as well as the least coercive outcome. Following this, Reder, Duncan and Gray's (1993) analysis of over 30 serious case reviews (SCRs), and later work by Reder and Duncan (1999), analysing over 100 SCRs, further developed the phenomenon of professional dangerousness. Munro has written that in more recent times patterns of professional dangerousness are referred to in Child Safeguarding Practice Reviews (previously Serious Case Reviews) in England and their equivalents in Wales, Scotland and Northern Ireland.

Psychology and systems thinking provide a range of theoretical ideas which help underpin and elucidate the concept of professional dangerousness. Interprofessional communication, for example, can be thought of as practical but also as psychological and relational, as safe practice can be how professionals process information available to them and how they think about and interact with others (Reder and Duncan, 2003). Psychologists and social workers have sought to understand heuristics and biases, as these can impact on the accuracy of professional judgement (Featherston et al., 2019; Kahneman, 2011). One example is confirmation bias, which is a tendency to seek, process and interpret information that is consistent with a pre-existing belief, rather than considering the full spectrum of available information (Spratt, Devaney and Hayes, 2015). This may be reflective of not listening carefully to what children say and do, concrete solutions, closure and operating a rule of optimism, for instance.

Systems theory is closely associated with ideas about professional dangerousness. Reder, Duncan and Gray (1993) took a systems approach to analyse over 30 SCRs, and in later work (Reder and Duncan, 1999), they analysed over 100 cases where children had died or been seriously harmed from abuse. It was through analysing evidence and thinking systemically that the authors were able to conceptualise the dynamic and interdependent nature of professional dangerousness. Systems theory describes how behaviour is influenced by a variety of factors working together to form a system and how different parts of the system are interconnected. Bateson (1972) is attributed with developing systemic ideas to recognise patterns of communication, beliefs, behaviours, roles, power structures and other social influences which maintain how a family functions.

Systems thinking encourages an acceptance that there are multiple truths, perspectives and possibilities and not focusing on a single 'presenting problem'. Systems approaches look to the wider system that perpetuates the 'problem' or undermines a solution, and it is through respectful curiosity (Cecchin, 1987), careful listening, exploration and hypothesising about behaviours and beliefs that systemic change can take place. Systems thinking also highlights the influence of structural and organisational contexts, and this resonates with Calder's (2008) position that professional dangerousness cannot be fully understood without thinking about the impact of organisational contexts. Burton and Revell (2018) also point to systemic and structural dimensions, such as the influence of political ideology, that can create barriers to professional curiosity, potentially creating the conditions for dangerous practice.

Applying the concepts to practice – using the checklist tool

One way to apply the concepts to professional practice is to record your understanding of each, along with any examples that you have come across in practice that you think may be relevant (Table 4.2). As you apply them to your subjective experiences, they are more likely to make sense to you and be more memorable. This exercise should support your understanding and recall of the concepts and analyse your intuitive feelings to evaluate underlying risks in the family and in relation to the professional system. You may also want to use other tools to support you to be professionally curious (Duckett, 2022, in Dix and Howells, 2022).

Table 4.2 Blank professional dangerousness checklist

Type of dangerousness	My understanding using examples from my practice or learning experience
Children and carers unheard	
Rule of optimism	
Concrete solutions	
Assessment paralysis	
Stereotyping and cultural relativity	
Closure/Avoidance	
Priority given to recent information	
Non-compliance with statutory procedures	
Role confusion	
Exaggeration of hierarchy	
Stockholm syndrome	
Omnipotence	
False or disguised compliance	
Professional accommodation syndrome	

Another way is to use the concepts as part of reflective discussions in peer groups, team meetings or in individual or group supervision. The concepts can also be used to analyse practice scenarios, chronologies, written records and referrals, as well as within professional network meetings, with inter-professional colleagues in health, education and police to explore and explain past and current decisions, tensions and actions. They may be used as prompts to discuss concerns with members of the child's or adult's personal network and to talk about worries that social workers have, which may support family members' understanding of professionals' concerns.

Practice application

The following account demonstrates the utility of the concepts from the perspective of a social work student who had heard about it for the first time. It is useful to point out that the quote was part of an ethically approved, unpublished pilot study and the student had experience of working in the social care sector prior to embarking on a qualifying social work course.

> *For me it was more shocking that I had not heard the term before and I think it is something that should span across not just social work but any health and care setting… now if I go into any situation I am thinking 'rule of optimism' I'm thinking ok, 'concrete solutions'. I'm thinking, am I just going for the easy option here or am I trying to see what's beyond this?*

The quote indicates that having an awareness and understanding of the concepts, as Calder (2008) suggests, offers a way of recognising and encouraging practitioners to look in greater depth, which promotes safe practice.

Professional dangerousness checklist questionnaire

As an example of how the concepts can be used, Table 4.3 below provides a series of questions and statements which work as prompts to encourage application to practice. Think about a child or adult you are working with, or have worked with, where there were or are existing concerns about risk and try to respond to the questions. Where you have indicated 'no' or 'maybe' should signal an opportunity to discuss the work and your intuitive feelings in more depth.

The **checklist** can be used individually or in formal supervision to analyse practice where there are concerns about risk to a child or adult. Supervision, as a space for critical reflection and emotional support (as well as managerial requirements), is an obvious opportunity for discussing professional dangerousness as part of

Table 4.3 Professional dangerousness yes/no checklist

Type of professional dangerousness	Questions to help identify potential professional dangerousness	Yes/I have/I am/I do	No/I do not/I have not	Maybe
Children or adults at risk and carers unheard	I respect the child's (or adult's) rights, wisdom and perspective.			
	I have listened carefully to the child (or adult) and parent/carer and the people they are most likely to have talked to about possible abuse? E.g. friends and neighbours?			
	Am I able to overcome emotional, organisational or other barriers to accessing the child's (or adult's) views and reality?			
	Do I ensure adult/carer perspectives are not overshadowing those of the child (or adult)?			
	I have systems and resources in place which I use to support me to look deeper and which challenge my thinking.			
Rule of optimism	I (and my colleagues) ensure I do not look for the more optimistic explanations without clear evidence.			
	I (and my colleagues) look for a full range of perspectives and am prepared to think the unthinkable and be professionally curious.			
	When I feel overwhelmed, I gain support to analyse risk situations in depth.			

(Continued)

Table 4.3 (*Continued*)

Type of professional dangerousness	Questions to help identify potential professional dangerousness	Yes/I have/I am/I do	No/I do not/I have not	Maybe
Concrete solutions:	The changes that are needed within a realistic timeframe have been clearly articulated and understood by everyone.			
	Am I satisfied that any material or practical support that is in place or being considered is going to bring about sufficient change and that this change can be measured?			
Assessment paralysis:	I am satisfied that I am able to gather relevant and accurate information to inform my assessment.			
	I feel hopeful in the situation and believe change is possible, as not everything has been tried.			
Stereotyping and cultural relativity:	I check my assumptions based on intersectional markers of identity, e.g. disability, class, ethnicity, religion, gender, sexual orientation and so on.			
	My colleagues and I seek and gain specialist advice and knowledge.			

(*Continued*)

Table 4.3 *(Continued)*

Type of professional dangerousness	Questions to help identify potential professional dangerousness	Yes/I have/I am/I do	No/I do not/I have not	Maybe
Closure/ Avoidance:	I evaluate how open and honest the family is about daily life experiences for the child (or adult client).			
	I actively pursue support to maintain contact with the family, despite feelings of fear and trepidation.			
	I am prepared to share with others that I feel afraid.			
	I have support and the resources I need to carry out visits despite my fears.			
	I am aware that seeking to appease parents and carers may be an unsafe practice.			
Priority given to recent information:	I complete or seek accurate chronologies which include the child's or adult's perspective on events.			
	I seek different views which challenge my perspective.			
	I am prepared to change my mind or acknowledge my mistakes.			
Non-compliance with statutory procedures:	I follow accurate and up-to-date procedures.			
	I try to stay updated on current practice and research.			

(Continued)

Table 4.3 *(Continued)*

Type of professional dangerousness	Questions to help identify potential professional dangerousness	Yes/I have/I am/I do	No/I do not/I have not	Maybe
Role confusion:	I am clear about my role and responsibilities and tasks, goals and timeframes.			
Exaggeration of hierarchy:	I regard the perspectives of experts or specialists to be equally valuable as those in informal positions or roles.			
	I can manage conflict.			
	I am confident in my professional opinion.			
Stockholm syndrome:	I am aware not to over-identify with parents/carers.			
	I remain focused on the child (adult client) and am aware not to get drawn into adults'/carers' concerns predominantly.			
	I am aware not to normalise parents or carers as victims.			

(Continued)

Table 4.3 (Continued)

Type of professional dangerousness	Questions to help identify potential professional dangerousness	Yes/I have/I am/I do	No/I do not/I have not	Maybe
Omnipotence:	I find it helpful to collaborate with others.			
	I do not establish special relationships with families and some professionals, more than other professionals.			
	My understanding of the family is not superior to that of other professionals.			
False or disguised compliance:	I look for real change taking place.			
	I am alert to the fact that a parent or carer may try and convince me of their cooperation despite there being little or no evidence of change?			
	I am aware that trying to be helpful by doing most or all the work may be unsafe practice.			
Professional accommodation syndrome:	Is there an opportunity in my team to share my 'gut' feelings?			
	When I share my thoughts and feelings about my concerns, I am respected and listened to by my peers and supervisor.			

respectful challenge. However, supervision can be a negative experience which can damage trust and belief in what supervision has the potential to offer, leading to defensiveness and an inability to acknowledge mistakes, doubts and fears (Morrison, 1990). One study of supervision (Hunt *et al.*, 2016) found that many workers felt inadequately supported, which negatively impacted their practice and the quality of protection provided to children. In view of this, the tools in this chapter could also be used within a peer-aided judgement model (Helm, 2022) to enhance critical thinking and collaborative and ethical decision-making.

The focus has primarily been on working with children and families, but there is a clear relevance to working with adults at risk, as highlighted in the introduction. Thematic analysis of Safeguarding Adult Reviews (SARs) (Braye and Preston-Shoot, 2020) identified several instances of professional dangerousness. Issues such as poor practice in transitional safeguarding, young people being placed in unregulated accommodation without proper risk assessments, and assumptions about mental capacity, coercive control, domestic abuse and self-neglect were noted, alongside a lack of professional challenge, biased thinking, and misinterpretations by workers. More professional curiosity could have led to interventions that might have prevented harm. Braye and Preston-Shoot's (2020, p. 134) analysis highlights that:

> *Cumulative and repeating patterns were not always identified or used to build understanding and were treated in isolation.*

> *[SARs] refer to a culture of professional optimism that prevented practitioners from looking beyond the presenting circumstances to address 'why' questions, and to a prioritisation of autonomy and lifestyle choice over risk and protection.*

> *One SAR attributes the lack of professional curiosity to factors such as time constraints, fear of offending, lack of cultural awareness, and a belief that other agencies were already handling these issues.*

These quotes illustrate how applying professional dangerousness concepts can support professional curiosity, fostering reflexive and critical analysis. Time pressure (including from high unmanageable caseloads) can lead to minimising abuse victims' experiences, making assumptions and operating a rule of optimism.

Three key points

- **Professional Dangerousness in Safeguarding**: The concept highlights some of the complex emotional and social interactions that take place in safeguarding practice organisations, prompting practitioners to consider how well-intentioned actions can sometimes unintentionally contribute to harm.

- **Interactive Checklists as Tools**: Two interconnecting checklists are presented to support practitioners to apply professional dangerousness concepts, promoting systemic analysis, professional curiosity and challenging assumptions and biases.
- **Collaboration and Multi-Agency Plans**: The chapter highlights that, in managing risk, no single tool or approach replaces well-resourced and well-supported individuals and teams, collaborating with other professionals and working in partnership with children and protective adults, to create robust, evidence-informed multi-agency plans that adhere to statutory guidelines.

REFERENCES

Allnock, D. and Miller, P. (2013) *No one noticed. No one heard. A study of disclosures of childhood abuse*. London: NSPCC.

Burton, V. and Revell, L. (2018) 'Professional curiosity in child protection: Thinking the unthinkable in a neo-liberal world', *British Journal of Social Work*, 48, pp. 1508–1523.

Bateson, G. (1972) *Steps to an ecology of mind*. New York: Ballantine Books.

Batty, D. (2002). 'Political correctness or poor practice?' *The Guardian Newspaper* [Online]. Available at https://www.theguardian.com/society/2002/mar/25/1 (Accessed 12 January 2025).

Bernard, C. (2019) 'Recognizing and addressing child neglect in affluent families', *Child and Family Social Work*, 24(2), pp. 340–347.

Brandon, M., Bailey, P., Belderson, R., Gardner, P., Sidebotham, J., Dodsworth, Warren, C. and Black, J. (2009) *Understanding serious case reviews and their impact: A biennial analysis of serious case reviews 2005-07*. London: DCSF.

Braye, S. and Preston-Shoot, M. (2020). *Analysis of Safeguarding Adult Reviews April 2017–March 2019* [Online]. Available at https://www.local.gov.uk/sites/default/files/documents/National%20SAR%20Analysis%20Final%20Report%20WEB.pdf (Accessed 13 January 2025).

Calder, M. (2008) *Contemporary risk assessment in safeguarding children*. Lyme Regis: Russell House.

Cecchin, G. (1987) 'Hypothesising, circularity and neutrality revisited: An invitation to curiosity', *Family Process*, 26, pp. 405–413.

Davies, J. (2022). 'Adultification bias within child protection and safeguarding'. *Academic Insights 2022/06*. HM Inspectorate of Probation [Online]. Available at https://cloud-platform-e218f50a4812967ba1215eaecede923f.s3.amazonaws.com/uploads/sites/32/2022/06/Academic-Insights-Adultification-bias-within-child-protection-and-safeguarding.pdf (Accessed 12 January 2025).

Davies, L. and Duckett, N. (2016) *Proactive child protection and social work*. 2nd edn. Exeter: SAGE Publications.

Dickens, J., Taylor, J., Cook, L., Cossar, J., Garstang, J., Hallett, N., Molloy, E., Rennolds, N., Rimmer, J., Sorensen, P. and Wate, R. (2022) *Learning for the future: Final analysis of serious case reviews, 2017 to 2019*. London: DFE.

Dingwall, R., Eekelaar, J. and Murray, T. (1983) *The protection of children: State intervention and family life*. Oxford: Blackwell.

Dingwall, R. (2013) 'The Rule of Optimism – Thirty Years On'. *Social Science Space* [Online]. Available at https://www.socialsciencespace.com/2013/09/the-rule-of-optimism-thirty-years-on/ (Accessed 21 January 2025).

Duckett, N. (2022). 'Exploring professional curiosity and social work practice education', in Dix, H. and Howells, A. (eds.) *Creative approaches to social work practice learning*. 1st edn. St Albans: Critical Publishing.

Featherston, R.J., Shlonsky, A., Lewis, C., Luong, M., Downie, L.E., Vogel, A.P., Granger, C., Hamilton, B. and Galvin, K. (2019) 'Interventions to mitigate bias in social work decision-making: A systematic review', *Research on Social Work Practice*, 29(7), pp. 741–752.

Ferguson, H. (2018) 'How children become invisible in child protection work: Findings from research into day-to-day social work practice', *The British Journal of Social Work*, 47(4), pp. 1007–1023, June 2017 (Accessed 1 November 2024).

Helm, D. (2011) 'Judgements or assumptions? The role of analysis in assessing children and young people's needs', *The British Journal of Social Work*, 41(5), pp. 894–911 (Accessed 19 January 2025).

Helm, D. (2022) 'Theorising social work sense-making: Developing a model of peer-aided judgement and decision making', *The British Journal of Social Work*, 52(4), pp. 2329–2347.

Hood, R. (2014) 'Complexity and integrated working in children's services', *The British Journal of Social Work*, 44(1), pp. 27–43.

Hunt, S., Goddard, C., Cooper, J., Littlechild, B. and Wild, J. (2016) 'If I feel like this, how does the child feel?" Child protection workers, supervision, management and organisational responses to parental violence', *Journal of Social Work Practice*, 30(1), pp. 5–24.

Independent Inquiry Child Sexual Abuse (IICSA) (2020). *"People Don't Talk about It": Child Sexual Abuse in Ethnic Minority Communities* [Online]. Available at https://www.iicsa.org.uk/reports-recommendations/publications/research/child-sexual-abuse-ethnic-minority-communities.html (Accessed 1 February 2025).

Julich, S. (2005) 'Stockholm syndrome and child sexual abuse', *Journal of Child Sexual Abuse*, 14(3), pp. 107–129.

Kahneman, D. (2011) *Thinking, fast and slow*. New York: Farrar, Straus and Giroux.

Kemshall, H. (2013). 'Risk assessment and risk management', in Davies, M. (ed.) *The Blackwell companion to social work*. 4th edn. London: Wiley Blackwell, pp. 333–342.

Kettle, M. and Jackson, S. (2017) 'Revisiting the rule of optimism', *The British Journal of Social Work*, 47(6), pp. 1624–1640.

Laming, L. (2003) *The Victoria Climbié inquiry. Report of an inquiry by Lord Laming*. Cm 5730. London: TSO.

Leigh, J., Beddoe, L. and Keddell, E. (2020) 'Disguised compliance or undisguised nonsense? A critical discourse analysis of compliance and resistance in social work practice', *Families, Relationships and Societies*, 9(2), pp. 269–285.

Littlechild, B. (2005) 'The nature and effects of violence against child-protection social workers: Providing effective support', *The British Journal of Social Work*, 35, pp. 387–401.

Littlechild, B. (2012). *Avoiding Avoidance Recognising and Responding to the Risks of Resistant and Uncooperative Parents in Child Protection* [Online]. Available at https://swscmedia.wordpress.com/2012/05/23/%E2%80%A8avoiding-avoidance-recognising-and-responding-to-the-risks-of-resistant-and-uncooperative-parents-in-child-protection-swscmedia-debate/ (Accessed 28 January 2025).

Mason, B. (2022) 'Towards positions of safe uncertainty', *Human Systems*, 2(2), pp. 54–63.

Merriam Webster Dictionary (2024). *Dangerousness* [Online]. Available at https://www. merriam-webster.com/dictionary/dangerousness (Accessed 25 January 2025).

Morris, K., Mason, W., Bywaters, P., Featherstone, B., Daniel, B., Brady, G., Hooper, J., Mirza, N., Scourfield, J. and Webb, C. (2018) 'Social work, poverty, and child welfare interventions', *Child and Family Social Work*, 23, pp. 364–72.

Morrison, T. (1990) 'The emotional effects of child protection work on the worker', *Practice*,, 4(4), pp. 253–271.

Munro, E. (1999) 'Comon errors of reasoning in child protection work', *Child Abuse and Neglect*, 23, pp. 745–758.

Munro, E. (2007) *Child protection*. 1st edn. London: SAGE.

Office of the Children's Commissioner (2015). *Protecting Children from Harm* [Online]. Available at https://assets.childrenscommissioner.gov.uk/wpuploads/2017/06/Protecting-children-from-harm-executive-summary_0.pdf (Accessed 20 January 2025).

Reder, D.P., Duncan, S. and Gray, M. (1993) *Beyond blame: Child abuse tragedies revisited*. 1st edn. Oxford: Routledge.

Reder, P. and Duncan, S. (1995) 'Closure, covert warnings, and escalating child abuse', *Child Abuse and Neglect*, 19(12), pp. 1517–1521.

Reder, P. and Duncan, S. (1999) *Lost innocents: A follow-up study of fatal child abuse*. Hove: Routledge.

Reder, P. and Duncan, S. (2003) 'Understanding communication in child protection networks', *Child Abuse Review*, 12(2), pp. 82–100 (Accessed 10 December 2024).

Spratt, T., Devaney, J. and Hayes, D. (2015) 'In and out of home care decisions: The influence of confirmation bias in developing decision-supportive reasoning', *Child Abuse and Neglect*, 49, pp. 76–85.

Summit, R.C. (1983) 'The child sexual abuse accommodation syndrome', *Child Abuse and Neglect*, 7, pp. 177–193.

Taylor, B.J. (2017) 'Heuristics in professional judgement: A psycho-social rationality model', *The British Journal of Social Work*, 47(4), pp. 1043–1060.

Taylor, J., Dickens, J., Garstang, J., Cook, L., Hallett, N. and Molloy, E. (2024) 'Tackling the "normalisation of neglect": Messages from child protection reviews in England', *Child Abuse Review*, 33(1), pp. 1–10.

Webb, E., Maddocks, A. and Bongilli, J. (2002) 'Effectively protecting black and minority ethnic children from harm: Overcoming barriers to the child protection process', *Child Abuse Review*, 11, pp. 394–410.

White, S. and Featherstone, B. (2005) 'Communicating misunderstandings: Multi-agency work as social practice', *Child and Family Social Work*, 10(3), pp. 207–216.

Chapter 5

From conflict to clarity: Navigating difficult conversations to assess and address risk

Shorolla Allen

As a social worker, to understand people's circumstances and effectively assess and address risk, you are required to discuss matters regarding safety, well-being and support needs with people who use services, colleagues and partner services. Although these discussions are an essential and vital part of the role, they usually involve sensitive topics and are therefore likely to elicit strong emotions and responses. It should come as no surprise then, that navigating difficult conversations can sometimes feel overwhelming, especially given that these conversations are often had during uncertain times and may have high-stake implications.

The consequences of ineffective communication during these times have been well-documented, particularly in relation to child fatalities (Laming, 2003, 2009; Munro, 2011). When social workers hesitate to discuss sensitive topics, they risk missing signs of possible harm, which can leave individuals, particularly children, without necessary support or place them at further risk; however, Munro (2011) offers the insight that, when handled with respect and transparency, "difficult" conversations can be a catalyst for building trust. Effective communication therefore remains foundational in ensuring vulnerable people receive the necessary support and protection (Healey, 2018). By engaging in self-reflection, social workers can develop greater awareness of their emotional triggers, biases and assumptions, which in turn can support them to communicate with empathy and improve social work outcomes even in diverse and challenging circumstances (Schön, 1983). This self-awareness is key in developing confidence when engaging in sensitive conversations, helping to foster collaboration and creating opportunities for meaningful discussions about risk and actions needed to move towards positive change.

This chapter offers three tools to aid the development of your reflective and relational practice. Tools 1 (see Figure 5.1) and 3 (see Figure 5.4) aim to help you gain a better awareness of yourself and reflect on how your experiences

DOI: 10.4324/9781041054740-6

may influence your approach and decision-making, while Tool 2 (see Figure 5.3) supports you to consider the lived experiences of individuals, providing a deeper understanding of their circumstances. It creates a space for you to reflect on these experiences and work through tangible actions that can support positive change, ensuring that interventions to address risk are both empathetic and effective.

TOOL 1: THE "SELF" TREE

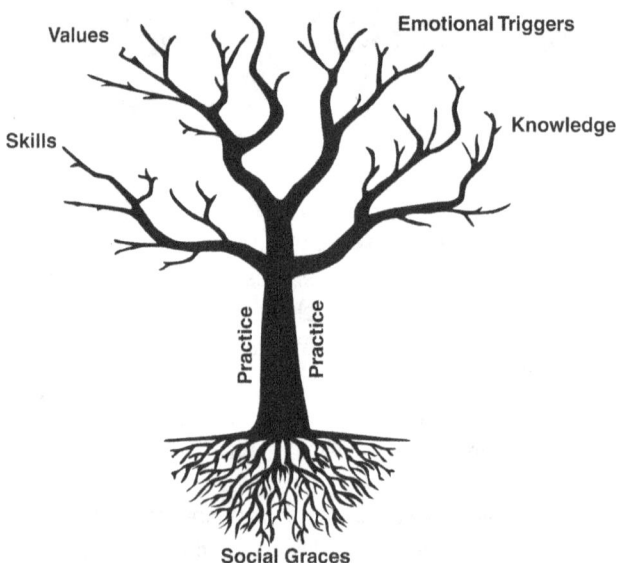

Figure 5.1 Tool 1 – The "Self" tree

Inspiration

My experiences of working directly with children and families inspired me to create the "Self" Tree. In a fast-paced child protection team, finding the time to sit back and reflect on what I was doing and why was never easy to do. My supervision sessions were predominately "case management"-focused – "dotting the I's and crossing the T's". I held no space for reflection, and as time went on, I came to the realisation that the less time I spent trying to understand what I was doing and why, the more I worried that I would start practising in a way that was driven by unintended shortcuts. At first, I didn't think anything of it until a heightened conversation happened with a parent who was upset because she didn't agree with the concerns I had for her child's safety. I found it challenging to navigate the conversation as I was trying to balance my responsibility to safeguard the child by voicing my concerns, whilst also maintaining a relationship with the parent to support positive change. I quickly realised that the outcome for this child was not only reliant on what I was doing, but how I was doing it, and the approach I took to discussing the sensitive topics during one of the most difficult times in this family's life. I then reprioritised time for reflection during supervision, focusing on "self" and the "use of self" and how my own experiences and biases could influence my views and/or approach to children and families.

Introduction to the tool

The "Self" Tree tool provides a creative and visual way to critically analyse what you bring to your practice as a social worker. This can apply more generally but also can be used to inform particular areas of practice such as the assessment of risk. It enables you to recognise your unconscious and conscious biases and emotional triggers, enabling more objective risk assessments and an evidence-based, compassionate approach.

The "Self" Tree has six elements to explore. The root of the tree explores your *social "GRACES"* e.g., age, ethnicity and gender. Each of the four branches explores a different area of reflection: your values, skills, knowledge and emotional triggers. The trunk of the tree supports you to reflect on how the roots and branches come together to influence your practice.

By examining your *social "GRACES"*, you can reflect on how your personal and professional characteristics and experiences shape your understanding of individuals and families, considering the impact of biases or cultural perspectives. Recognising your *values* ensures alignment with professional standards and encourages transparency when navigating ethical dilemmas. Exploring *emotional triggers* helps to identify your emotional responses that might affect objectivity or escalate situations. Assessing *skills and knowledge* highlights areas of competence and gaps, ensuring informed and effective interventions.

THE SOCIAL *"GRACES"*

G – Gender, geography

R – Race, religion

A – Age, ability, appearance

C – Class, culture

E – Ethnicity, employment, education

S – Sexuality, sexual orientation, spirituality

Theory

To facilitate meaningful conversations about risk, it's firstly important to recognise and understand that risk can be perceived differently by different people and services. The *social "GRACES"* framework (Burnham, 2012) can be used as a means to explore and understand the diverse and intersecting aspects of identity that can shape culture, experiences, biases and perceptions of risk. It can provide you with a structured way to think about how identity and power can shape both communication and relationships.

Building on the *social "GRACES"* framework, this tool moves beyond reflective practice into reflexive practice, encouraging not only evaluation of past actions and experiences but also ongoing awareness of how biases, emotions and perspectives shape decision-making and interactions in the present. Reflexive practice is significant because it allows you to adapt your approach in real time, promoting a deeper understanding of power dynamics, biases and systematic influences (Fook and Gardner, 2007).

How to use the tool

Ideally, this tool is to be utilised as a reflexive tool within supervision. Simply use **the "Self" Tree** to develop insight about what you bring to your social work practice. The template is intentionally simple, and I would recommend adding other topic(s) or characteristics to your "branches", "roots" or "leaves", that you may find helpful to explore. I encourage you to use this tool to think about how each section may influence your "trunk", shaping your perceptions, interactions and relationships with the people you work with.

I would recommend you print this tool as A3 or larger. The tool can also be laminated for multiple uses – simply take a picture of your reflections once you are done.

The prompts below can be used as a guide to reflect on each section. The sections can be considered independently, or you can work through them all in any sequence.

Social "GRACES"

- How do your characteristics influence your interactions with others?
- Which of your traits do you feel most proud of? How do they impact your personal/professional relationships?

Values

- What are the top three values that guide your decisions and behaviour?
- Are there any areas where your personal values conflict with your professional duties? How do you navigate these conflicts?

Emotional Triggers

- What situations or behaviours trigger strong emotional reactions in you? Why?
- Can you think of a time when your values were challenged? How did you respond?

Skills and Knowledge

- What skills do you feel most confident in? How do you use them in your work or daily life?
- Are there any areas of knowledge you'd like to develop further? Why are these important to you?
- Can you think of a time when your skills or knowledge made a significant difference in a situation?
- What strategies do you use to share your knowledge and skills with others?

Figure 5.2 below demonstrates how I successfully used this tool with a first-year social work student to help her gain insight into how her strong value of honesty influenced her practice with individuals she believed were lying. In instances she felt she was being lied to, she was more likely to seek evidence to prove they were lying rather than to confirm that they were telling the truth. After understanding this, she recognised the need to adopt a more balanced approach by actively considering evidence that could support both perspectives.

Other ways to use the tool

This tool can also be used within group supervision conversations. It can offer an opportunity for supervisors/team managers to guide team members to reflect on their organisational attitudes to risk and the ways in which this may influence their team/service approach to practice. It can also be used to explore and understand instances of differing professional judgements between practitioner and manager. This can be done by using 1:1 conversations, feedback or observations to reflect on where values align or conflict.

transparency honesty **Values**

Emotional Triggers injustice

Family trust

???

Knowledge

Skills

Relation

??? social work

Collaboration

monitoring level
3

Report ???????

??? ??? ??? ???

ampatiac??

romm????? Aud?????

Practice Practice

Female

Small town

Christian 21

B/w
????????

Social Graces

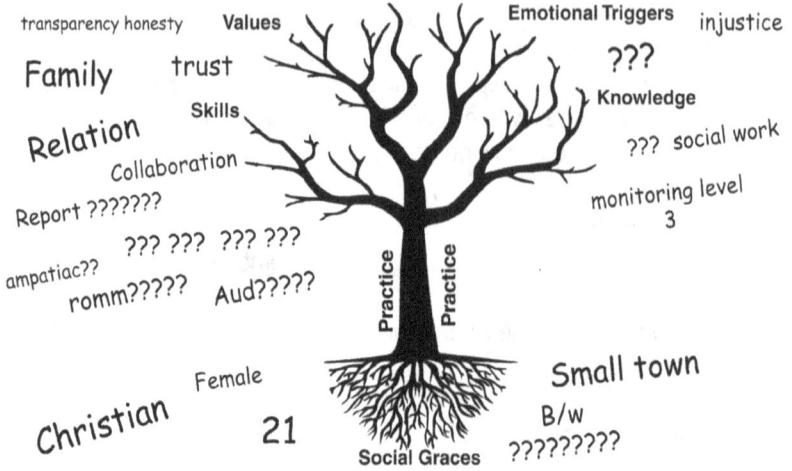

Figure 5.2 Annotated "Self" tree

Note to supervisor:

For this activity to be most effective when done in a supervision setting, it's crucial to create a safe, non-judgmental space where the practitioner feels comfortable exploring these issues.

TOOL 2: THE TRIPLE TAKE TOOL

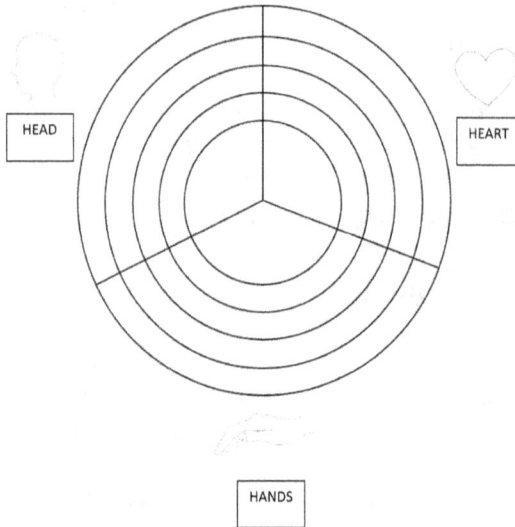

HEAD

HEART

HANDS

Figure 5.3 Tool 2 – The triple take tool

Inspiration

My inspiration for this tool stems from a deep desire to help people navigate the complexities of addressing risk with compassion and clarity. After receiving bespoke training from the influential Karen Treisman, the principle she discussed, "connection before correction", has always resonated with me and remained a guiding principle for my work. The idea that we cannot influence positive change until we connect with people, creating a sense of openness and safety. The hope for this tool is to inspire a deeper understanding and connection with the people and systems around us, helping social workers to approach conversations and decisions about risk in both a meaningful and transformative way.

Introduction to tool

Within social work practice it is important to acknowledge that people do not operate in isolation but as part of a wider system. The **"Triple Take"** tool provides a holistic approach to exploring people's circumstances when assessing and responding to risk. This tool will be helpful when working directly with people with lived experience, to provide a structured framework to organise conversations, ensuring all critical elements – evidence, feelings and actions – are identified and addressed systematically and through a systems theory lens. This model can support with reducing tension by making discussions feel purposeful and balanced. By exploring emotions and values, the tool acknowledges the feelings of all involved and encourages reflection on how these different perspectives and responses to risk influence people's experiences and outcomes. This can nurture trust and mutual respect, making it easier to address sensitive topics about risk. Considering the "head" and "heart" in tandem ensures that approaches taken are both evidence-informed and compassionate. This can help de-escalate conflicts rooted in misunderstanding or differing priorities. By bringing these components together to focus on actionable steps (hands), the tool helps social workers move conversations beyond disagreements to focus on collaborating on constructive solutions, empowering all parties to take positive steps forward.

Theory

This tool helps you to explore the interconnected aspects of the head, heart and hands model (Sipos, Battisti and Grimm, 2008) through the lens of ecological systems theory. The model emphasises the integration of evidence (head), emotions and values (heart) and practical actions (hands) in professional practice. It encourages a holistic approach by aligning critical thinking, empathy and effective action to achieve meaningful outcomes.

This model aligns effectively with Bronfenbrenner's (1979) ecological systems theory, by recognising the influence of multiple environmental layers on an individual's thoughts, emotions and actions. As a social worker you are tasked with navigating these multiple systems, ensuring the protection and well-being of the individual and others, whilst also understanding the complexities and pressures that families face. This is no easy task, as building a strong trusting relationship with anyone requires a display of solidarity and understanding. So, how do you demonstrate this when the actions you may need to take are perceived as demonstrating the opposite?

Bronfenbrenner's ecological systems theory identifies five nested systems:

• Microsystem – direct environment (individual, work, school, family, friends)
• Mesosystem – interactions between microsystems
• Exosystem – indirect influences like workplace polices or community resources
• Macrosystem – larger cultural or societal values that shape our experiences
• Chronosystem – how things change over time, like life stages or historical events.

Linking the two frameworks can provide deeper understanding of how to navigate difficult conversations about risk by considering the broader systematic context.

How to use the tool

This tool can be used with a person with lived experience as part of the assessment process, to gain a deeper understanding of their perspective, needs and factors influencing their situation. It can also be used to support transparent and collaborative conversations with individuals with lived experience, helping them work with you to create person-centred and solution-focused plans to reduce risk of harm to themselves or others.

By considering the questions below, you can not only assess risk but also develop empathetic, realistic actions that address the individual's needs and difficulties within each system level. The innermost circle represents the microsystem, which has the most direct and immediate influence on an individual, and the four remaining systems – mesosystem, exosystem, macrosystem and chronosystem – expanding outward, to reflect broader situational and environmental influences.

Head:

- **Microsystem:** What evidence of risk/need is there? Are there any signs of neglect, abuse or living in an unsafe living environment?
- **Mesosystem:** How do different systems interact to influence this risk/need?
- **Exosystem:** What factors such as community resources are inducing or reducing risk/need? Are they being affected by lack of support services? Or by factors beyond their control, like financial instability?
- **Macrosystem:** Are there cultural or societal norms affecting decision-making? Or how risk is viewed? How do broader societal or cultural attitudes such as stigma around mental health affect the individual?
- **Chronosystem:** Have risks evolved over time? Are there any significant life events, such as trauma, a change in family structure, or shift in community or societal conditions influence the risk?

Heart:

- **Microsystem:** How does the individual feel within their immediate environment? Are they anxious or confident?
- **Mesosystem:** How does the individual feel about the interactions between these environments? Are they overwhelmed by conflicting demands, or do they feel unsupported due to the tension between different areas in their life?
- **Exosystem:** How does the individual feel about the factors affecting them? Do they feel empowered? Are they frustrated, do they feel powerless or anxious or feel a lack of control over the systems?
- **Macrosystem:** Does the individual feel marginalised or have they been discriminated against? What emotions do they feel when confronted with societal or cultural pressures?
- **Chronosystem:** How do past experiences or ongoing changes shape the individual's emotional response to risk? Are they feeling more vulnerable or hopeful?

Hands:

- **Microsystem:** How can we create a safe, supportive space for the individual to express their feelings and concerns? What practical steps can be taken to address any immediate threats to safety?
- **Mesosystem:** How can we support communication between the different environments/systems to reduce tension/conflict? What strategies can

we implement to provide balance and support in different aspects of the individual's life?

- **Exosystem:** What steps can be taken to help the individual navigate and access available community resources or support services? How can you empower the individual to have more control or choice over their situation?
- **Macrosystem:** How can you challenge societal attitudes? Or work to reduce stigma? What can you do to help the individual feel validated and supported within their cultural context?
- **Chronosystem:** How can you acknowledge the impact of past experiences while encouraging hope and growth for the future? What interventions can be put in place to support the individual through life transitions and mitigate the effects of past trauma?

As you use this tool, take the time to explore any patterns of connection or differences between the systems and sections. Consider how the head, heart and hands are influenced by the systems surrounding the individual. Do you notice any recurring themes such as how external policies (exosystem) influence the individuals' access to resources? Identifying these patterns can help you better understand how different layers of influence intersect and guide you towards more balanced decisions that integrate evidence, empathy and solution-focused actions.

A colleague used this tool with "Jane" to aid her assessment to establish if the threshold had been met to support her and her three children (aged 11, 9 and 3) under S.17 of the Children Act 1989. Jane was experiencing ongoing conflict within her romantic relationship (a key element of the microsystem) which contributed to her heightened stress and use of alcohol. This stress was affecting her attendance and performance at work (mesosystem), and she would often call in sick and take long periods of time off work. Jane told me that she had attempted to access services to address what was happening to her, however, due to service demand, there was no immediate service available (exosystem). Jane shared feelings of being frustrated and let down because of this. Jane recognised that she was experiencing difficulties with her mental health and could sometimes find it difficult to get out of bed in the morning or perform simple, everyday tasks like brushing her teeth. Jane said that she felt she was not able to seek support for her mental health due to fears of being judged and her perception was that professionals would question her ability to safely care for her children. This fear fed into her use of alcohol – as a way to cope with the big feelings and stress she was experiencing. By acknowledging the wider and interconnecting systems and how this influenced Jane's circumstances, the social worker was not only able to identify the family's support needs, to keep the children safe, but also established a trusting and open relationship whereby Jane was more willing to engage in the assessment process and she felt empowered to make positive change for herself and her children.

Other ways to use the tool

This tool is not only helpful for assessing and responding to risk, but it can also be used proactively to anticipate influences before they happen. It allows you to explore potential challenges and risks by considering how different systems, perspectives, emotions etc. can shape a situation. In addition, this tool can be used after an interaction or decision has been made to evaluate and learn from those experiences, helping to refine future actions. Managers can also use this tool with their teams to explore live case supervision as a team, fostering thoughtful discussion and actions, supporting teams to collectively hold anxieties and risks when working with families and individuals with complex circumstances.

TOOL 3: EMOTIONAL RESPONSES CARDS

Fish out of water	Steering the ship	The storm will pass
Throw me a lifeline	Drifting in the tide	Crashing Wave
Steady waters	Focused on your own course	Create your own

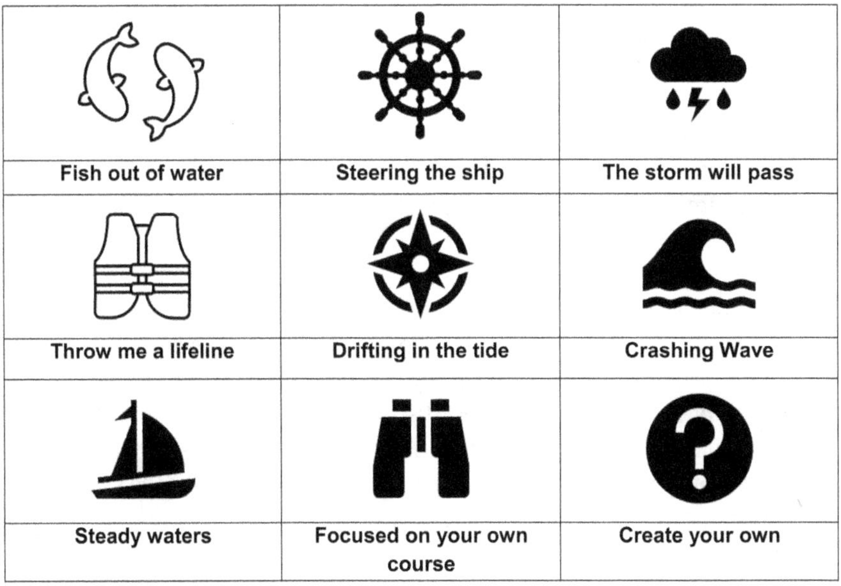

Figure 5.4 Tool 3 – Emotional responses cards

Introduction to the tool

Assessing and responding to risk in social work often involves challenging situations that can trigger strong emotions, such as dealing with trauma, mental health crisis, violence, abuse and various forms of vulnerability. Ferguson (2018) has noted that social workers can sometimes feel paralysed by the emotional impact of hostile relationships, which can limit their ability to think clearly and make effective decisions. The **Emotional Response Cards** are designed to be a visual and interactive tool to help you, and where appropriate, those with lived experience, recognise and understand how you respond to emotional triggers and responses. They serve as conversation starters about how your emotions shape your behaviour and decision-making, particularly in the context of assessing risk. This tool is invaluable in practice as it can support you to nurture deeper understanding of the people you are working with, enhance your emotional literacy and support interventions, tailored to people's specific emotional needs. Equally, the **Emotional Responses Cards** can help bridge gaps in communication, build rapport and encourage self-reflection.

The dialogue below provides further explanation of each card.

> **Fish out of water**: You lack confidence in having conversations that challenge or conversations that may be challenging. You often feel like you don't know what to say or how to say it.
> **Steering the ship**: You find it uncomfortable when you feel unable to control the decisions and outcomes for the people you are working with. If you perceive their decisions to be steering them away from your ideal "destination", you find it difficult to offer support.
> **The storm will pass**: You avoid conversations that may be difficult with the hopes that the "storm will pass".
> **Throw me a lifeline**: When conversations become difficult unexpectedly, you hope for someone to come and "save" you.
> **Drifting in the tide**: You prefer support for the initial steps of the difficult conversations, and then you believe you can manage the rest on your own.
> **Crashing wave**: If you are approached with conflict, you will likely react in kind, matching the intensity of the individual's interactions/response.
> **Steady waters:** You remain calm and composed, even when the situation becomes challenging.
> **Focused on your own course:** You might overlook the broader perspective because you're primarily focused on your own thoughts and feelings.

Inspiration

I created these cards with the conviction that emotional self-awareness is a powerful tool for personal and professional growth, especially for social workers who face emotionally charged situations daily. It's easy to become overwhelmed by the emotional weight of the work we do – whether it's dealing with risk, trauma, abuse or conflict. I wanted to offer a way for practitioners to pause, reflect and understand their emotional triggers, so they can respond with more clarity, empathy and effectiveness. By helping you recognise your emotional reactions, these cards provide a space for self-reflection and growth, allowing you to approach challenging situations with greater resilience and confidence. Ultimately, my goal was to create an easy to use, practical resource that empowers you to manage your emotions, strengthen your professional relationships and continue doing the important, life-changing work you do.

Theory

Emotional intelligence refers to the ability to recognise, understand and manage one's own emotions, as well as to perceive and influence the emotions of others. Central to emotional intelligence is self-awareness, self-regulation, empathy and social skills, which are essential for navigating complex interpersonal and professional scenarios (Goleman, 1995). These emotional responses cards align closely with emotional intelligence theory by providing a structured way to enhance self-awareness and reflection.

How to use the tool

Print, individually cut and laminate the cards. This tool can be used independently, within supervision or as part of a team/group activity.

Step one: Shuffle the deck of cards and place them in a pile **OR** scatter all of the cards face down on the table. **Select** the top card or a card at random.
Step two: Read the card and accompanying dialogue. Take a moment to pause and reflect. Think about a situation that triggered this emotional response.
Step three: Consider what triggered your emotional response – was it something specific about the person, interaction, environment that sparked this?

Ask yourself: What was it about this situation that made me feel this way?

Step four: Reflect on how your emotions influenced your behaviour. Did they shape your actions in a positive or negative way? How did they affect your decision-making or communication with others?
Step five: Think about how you might handle similar situations differently. What strategies could you use to make your emotions strong effectively?
Step six: Write down your reflections; writing helps solidify your insights and allows you to track your emotional growth over time. If working in a group or during supervision, discuss your reflections with others.

The **emotional response cards** were used by an experienced youth justice
practitioner within a supervision setting to explore their experiences. The example
illustrates the practitioners' reflections using the cards and the implications for
their practice.

Situation: Presenting for the first time in a Multi-Agency
Public Protection Arrangements (MAPPA) meeting.

Trigger: I was feeling overwhelmed by the complexity and
seriousness of public protection concerns.

Emotional response: I had increased anxieties. *Limited contribution
to the meeting.*

Reflection on potential implications to practice: Other professionals could lose confidence in my ability to support this child. This could
lead to a breakdown in effective communication between professionals
which could cause unclear or poorly informed outcomes.

Following this, the practitioner found it helpful to consider how they could
overcome the challenges they faced, identifying strategies and actions to improve
their practice.

Other ways to use the tool

You may also want to create and add your own emotion cards e.g., anger, sadness
to your deck. Using these cards, you can pair your emotions to your emotional
response to gain insight into how your specific emotions shape your responses.

Key reflections

1   Think about what personal experiences, values and biases you bring to
    your practice. How do they shape the way you perceive and respond to
    situations? How might reflecting on these influences positively influence your
    decision-making?
2   How aware are you of your emotional triggers in practice? How do these
    emotions impact your relationships and decisions? What steps can you
    take to reflect on and manage these triggers to enhance your professional
    responses?

3   When assessing risk, how can you balance evidence, emotional and actionable steps to ensure your interventions are both person-centred and solution-focused? How might using a more structured approach help you remove personal bias and improve collaborative decision-making?

REFERENCES

Bronfenbrenner, U. (1979) *The ecology of human development: Experiments by nature and design*. Cambridge, MA: Harvard University Press.

Burnham, J. (2012). 'Developments in social GRRRAAACCEEESSS: Visible-invisible and voiced-unvoiced', in Krause, I.-B. (ed.) *Culture and reflexivity in systemic psychotherapy: Mutual perspectives*. London: Karnac Books, pp. 139–160.

Children Act (1989). London: The Stationery Office. Available at: https://www.legislation.gov.uk/ukpga/1989/41/section/17 [Accessed 26 November 2024].

Ferguson, H. (2018) 'How social workers engage with children and families: Relationship-based practice in action', *Child & Family Social Work*, 23(3), pp. 337–345.

Fook, J. and Gardner, F. (2007) *Practising critical reflection; A resource handbook*. Maidenhead: McGraw-Hill Education/Open University Press.

Goleman, D. (1995) *Emotional intelligence: Why it can matter more than IQ*. New York: Bantam Books.

Healey, C. (2018) *Effective communication in child protection social work*. London: Routledge.

Laming, H. (2003) *The Victoria Climbié inquiry: Report of an inquiry by Lord Laming*. London: The Stationery Office.

Laming, H. (2009) *The protection of children in England: A progress report*. London: The Stationery Office.

Munro, E. (2011) *The Munro review of child protection: Final report – A child-centred system*. London: Department for Education.

Schön, D.A. (1983) *The reflective practitioner: How professionals think in action*. New York: Basic Books.

Sipos, Y., Battisti, B. and Grimm, K. (2008) 'Achieving transformative sustainability learning: Engaging head, hands and heart', *International Journal of Sustainability in Higher Education*, 9, pp. 68–86. doi:10.1108/14676370810842193.

Chapter 6

Integrating therapeutic techniques into social work practice

Sophie Walters and Dhriti Sarkar

INTRODUCTION

This chapter explores the integration of therapeutic techniques into social work, providing a comprehensive guide for practitioners looking to elevate their practice and address risk. The value of therapy in social work is substantial, particularly of note is the way in which practitioners establish relationships with the individuals they work with. These relationships are characterised by empathy, openness and a non-judgemental approach. Central to this practice is a sense of curiosity, both about the people we work with and ourselves which underpins all three tools presented in this chapter. By incorporating methods traditionally associated with therapy, social workers can foster stronger relationships, mitigate risk, improve outcomes of their work and facilitate meaningful change. This chapter is structured around three tools: **'finding the hidden links'**, **'accepting feedback with open arms'** and **'building the foundations for good endings'**.

The **finding the hidden links** tool involves identifying the recurring patterns and central themes in an individual's narrative. By recognising these links, you can help people to make sense of their story, potentially shedding new light on their experiences. Practitioners can also tailor their interventions more effectively, ensuring that they address the root causes of an individual's challenges. This section will provide a practical strategy for identifying these patterns and

DOI: 10.4324/9781041054740-7

integrating this into the assessment and intervention processes. The tool can also be used to uncover previously unrecognised risks, helping to voice these with curiosity and empathy in a way that facilitates further exploration.

Feedback is a critical component of effective social work practice, yet it is often underutilised or mishandled. It is important to embrace feedback from people with lived experience, colleagues and supervisors. **Accepting feedback with open arms** is also about reframing how we receive negative feedback. We will explore how we perceive this and how this can be used to create stronger, more open relationships. This technique can help mitigate the risk of undermining integrity of the working relationship, by directly addressing the doubts and apprehensions of either party and thereby leaving space to communicate more freely in a way that is not road-blocked with unsaid fears and resentments. The chapter explores methods for creating a feedback-friendly environment where individuals feel comfortable sharing their thoughts and practitioners are open to receiving and acting on constructive criticism. We will also consider the role of reflective practice in personal and professional growth.

The conclusion of a relationship or intervention can be a pivotal moment in social work. **Building the foundations for good endings** focuses on working with endings right the way through our work and considering how both an individual's and our own experiences of previous endings can shape how we respond to these. Endings that are handled with care can provide closure and empower individuals to move forward. Risk must also be considered within these endings as it has the potential to undermine or destroy the progress that has been made. Preparing for an ending, celebrating progress, self-reflection and addressing any unresolved issues will all be thought about. By mastering the art of ending relationships positively, social workers can leave a lasting impact on the people they work with.

By bridging the gap between therapy and social work, this chapter aims to equip practitioners with the skills necessary to navigate the complexities of their role with empathy, insight and professionalism.

FINDING THE HIDDEN LINKS TOOL

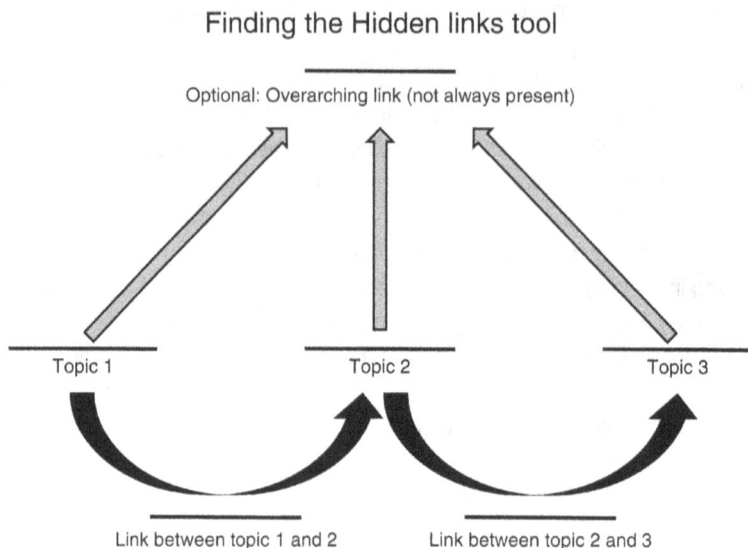

Finding the Hidden links tool

Optional: Overarching link (not always present)

Topic 1   Topic 2   Topic 3

Link between topic 1 and 2   Link between topic 2 and 3

> **Points to remember:**
>
> **Examples of open-ended questions:**
> • What would you like to explore today?
> • What is on your mind?
> • What would you like to focus on in our time together today?
> • How have things been going for you since we last spoke?
>
> **When identifying links:**
> - Listen to what is being said and the feelings and sentiments behind this – are there common themes?
> - Ask yourself – Why are they telling me this? Why now?
> - You can ask directly about the link between two topics if this is not clear to you
> - Consider what they may be trying to convey and what may be unspoken
>
> **When reflecting back what you have heard – keep it tentative:**
> ❖ It sounds like you are saying….
> ❖ Can I just check my understanding…
> ❖ I may have misunderstood but…
> ❖ I get the sense that you might be feeling …

Figure 6.1 Finding the hidden links tool

Inspiration

When I started practicing as a psychotherapist, I spent a lot of time listening to the people I worked with (indeed, we are very often advised to say less and listen more as trainees). I noticed that, when given the opportunity to speak freely, they moved between different topics, thoughts and ideas. While sometimes the reason for this shift in focus was immediately obvious, at other times, I found this harder to uncover. Initially, I would be unsure what linked two seemingly unrelated ideas.

I would frequently direct my curiosity towards the link between these different thoughts, including by asking directly about this and I almost always learnt something from this process. This method helped to stabilise me and prevented me getting lost in the overwhelming detail of the narratives presented to me.

I came to realise that the people I worked with were relating different concepts to me that were sometimes not linked directly by what they were saying but instead by a repeated feeling or experience. I came to understand that, more often than not, there was an association present in their minds when they moved between topics in this way. I found that for those with neurodiversity understanding, these links were particularly important as they had become accustomed to others failing to recognise links that seemed obvious in their mind. Uncovering these links and being able to voice it to the individual helped them make sense of their own story and shed new light on their experiences. By speaking about these links, I found I was able to move the work to a deeper level, reaching the essence of someone's narrative more quickly and directly, while forming a more meaningful relationship with them in the process – one in which they felt both heard and understood. I found this technique useful in orientating myself and refer to this as **finding the hidden links.** *People with lived experience often responded to this process with relief – they could sense that they were with someone who was actively thinking about them and trying to understand what they were conveying.*

Introduction to the tool

Many of the people we work with may have experiences of not being heard or have encountered injustice. They may be nervous about the intervention from a social worker and this may be expressed through talking a lot, trying to get their point across. Sometimes it can feel difficult to get through the surface detail to something deeper and more meaningful. The hidden links exist whether or not you can see them – they join different concepts and insights together in a cohesive and seamless way. **Finding the hidden links** tool (Figure 6.1) helps to uncover the central themes and recurring patterns. When using this tool, initially the hidden links can be jotted down in the form of mind map as shown in the images. As you become more skilled at using this, you may be able to visualise the links in your mind in real time as you sit with someone. The understanding should always be checked with the individual, as it is possible that the wrong conclusions may be drawn. The hidden links may also be in what is missing from someone's account and may help to draw attention to areas that would otherwise have been overlooked. Finding these links may allow a more empowering and coherent narrative to be created. Using this tool practitioners and supervisors can tailor their interventions more effectively, ensuring that they are addressing the root causes of the client's or supervisee's challenges as well as considering risks that may be present.

Theory

This technique draws on the concept of free association (Freud, 1913). Free association is a psychoanalytic method for exploring the unconscious mind. The individual speaks freely about whatever thoughts come to mind, without censorship or filtering. This technique aims to uncover thoughts and feelings that may be influencing current behaviour and emotions. The technique allows for spontaneous expression which helps to bypass conscious defences. By following seemingly random associations, the practitioner can identify patterns, themes and connections that reveal unconscious conflicts, desires and traumas. The aim is to listen for recurring themes that may indicate deeper or unconscious issues. The practitioner may then offer interpretations to help the individual to gain insight into these unconscious processes. The aim is to increase someone's insight into themselves.

Finding the hidden links involves listening on two levels, to both the 'manifest' and 'latent' content of the narrative (Freud, 1900). The former is the literal words that are being said and while the latter involves the deeper psychological meaning behind these words. This is not a new concept within psychotherapy, but it takes a good deal of practice to do well. You need to shift your focus back and forth between what is being said and the emotions behind this without losing track of either one of these strands.

How to use the tool

In order to use this tool, it is important to allow people to speak as freely as possible and not just to ask them a series of questions one after the other. Start with an open-ended question and give them the time and space to respond fully allowing them to move uninterrupted between topics. Remember that as they do so, you are listening on two levels – to both what is being said and the feelings and sentiment behind this.

Write down the two topics (or as you become more skilled, hold them in your mind). Try to find the link between them. Keep returning to asking yourself 'Why are they telling me this?' 'Why now?' Then attempt to draw the links between these topics – try to find the central themes and emotions. Reflect these links back – always do this in a tentative way and be prepared for them to tell you that you have missed the mark. You also need to think about what might not be being said.

Explore the link with them and again give them the space to respond freely to this. Follow where they move to after this link has been made – it may be that you can link the next topic to this as well. Through using empathy, curiosity and thinking together with people in a collaborative way previously unspoken risks may be identified.

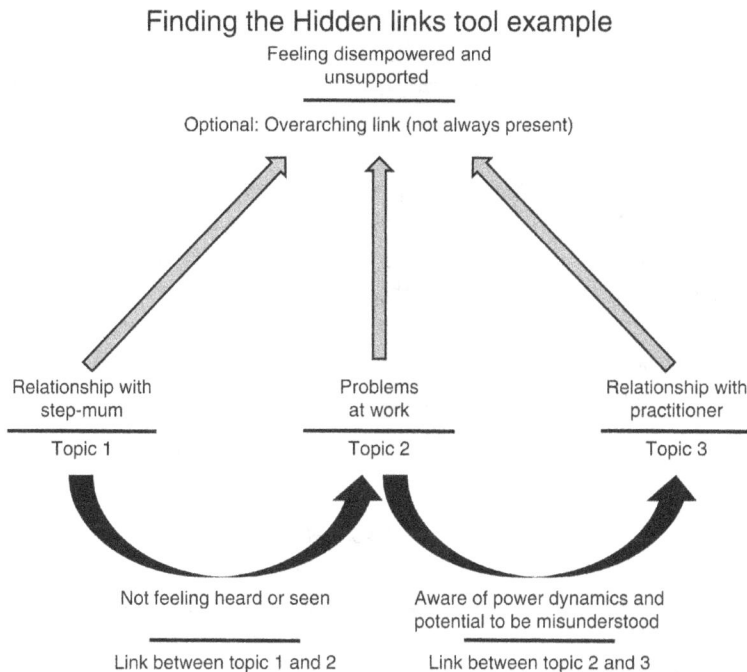

Finding the Hidden links tool example

Feeling disempowered and
unsupported

Optional: Overarching link (not always present)

Relationship with step-mum	Problems at work	Relationship with practitioner
Topic 1	Topic 2	Topic 3

Not feeling heard or seen   Aware of power dynamics and
potential to be misunderstood

Link between topic 1 and 2   Link between topic 2 and 3

Points to remember:

Examples of open-ended questions:
- What would you like to explore today?
- What is on your mind?
- What would you like to focus on in our time together today?
- How have things been going for you since we last spoke?

When identifying links:
- Listen to what is being said and the feelings and sentiments behind this – are there common themes?
- Ask yourself – Why are they telling me this? Why now?
- You can ask directly about the link between two topics if this is not clear to you
- Consider what they may be trying to convey and what may be unspoken

When reflecting back what you have heard – keep it tentative:
- ❖ It sounds like you are saying….
- ❖ Can I just check my understanding…
- ❖ I may have misunderstood but…
- ❖ I get the sense that you might be feeling …

Figure 6.2 Finding the hidden links tool example

Please see the example in Figure 6.2: I sat with an individual that I have been working with for some time. He is upset and begins to tell me about an incident with his step-mum (Topic 1) over the weekend. He went to visit her and she made derogatory comments about him, leaving him feeling bad about himself. She also complained bitterly about him to his sister, despite him doing his best to help her.

He then transitions into talking about his job (Topic 2). The project he is leading is not going well and he is upset that his boss has not provided more assistance to him with this. He has tried to outline the difficulties to his boss but this has fallen on deaf ears.

I would then direct my curiosity towards the link between Topics 1 and 2 in his mind. His relationship with his step-mum is strained and he feels overlooked, unheard and that he is treated like a problem. He also struggles at work feeling that people don't understand him and that he is not receiving the support that he so desperately needs. Rather than getting caught up in the intimate detail of the narratives about the specific incidents with his step-mum and at work, I am able to get to something much deeper. Not feeling heard or seen (Link A) is the common thread between these two topics. I voice this link to him that he briefly acknowledges this before moving on to talk about our therapeutic relationship.

When he speaks about our relationship, I wonder again about what the link might be (between Topics 2 and 3) and what he might be finding difficult to say. I consider with him whether it is possible that he is conscious of the power dynamics at play within our relationship and worries about being misunderstood? When I gently ask about this, he tells me that he sometimes worries that I won't hear him in the way that he hopes – this is much closer to the core of his experience. Through this we are able to speak to something delicate which otherwise he might have found difficult to raise. As part of this discussion, the client was able to tell me that he had considered not attending our sessions because of this fear. Through this I was able to explore and minimise the risk of non-engagement.

I then explore with him that in all three situations (Topics 1, 2 and 3) he feels disempowered and unsupported. This is a central theme for him and forms the overarching link within the discussion. By identifying this we are able to explore strategies to overcome this, using a solution-focused approach.

Other ways to use the tool

Students on placement may also feel overwhelmed and may bring an aspect of this to supervision, presenting with many disparate ideas and thoughts. Practice educators can use this tool to help ground the students and focus on the issues that are most important to them. Students can also benefit from experiencing this tool themselves before using it out in practice. Through using this method, practice educators can help students to feel heard on a deeper level and can enhance their practice by getting to core issues and feelings more directly. Expressing these links to the student can help them develop their own self-awareness and they may also become conscious of how aspects of their own experience may become reignited in their work. This tool can help form a more meaningful supervisory relationship and allow the student to bring their full self to their role as a social worker.

Three key takeaway messages

1   Identifying Underlying Themes: Finding hidden links allows practitioners to uncover central themes and recurring patterns. This method helps to connect disparate topics through shared emotions or experiences, providing a deeper understanding of an individual's narrative.
2   Enhanced Therapeutic Relationship: By recognising and articulating these hidden links, practitioners can deepen their relationship with the people they work with. This approach fosters a sense of being truly heard and understood, which can enhance effectiveness and create a more collaborative and therapeutic environment.
3   Tailored Interventions: Understanding the hidden links between various aspects of the story enables practitioners to tailor interventions more effectively. Addressing these core themes helps in targeting the root causes of challenges rather than just the surface issues.

ACCEPTING FEEDBACK WITH OPEN ARMS TOOL

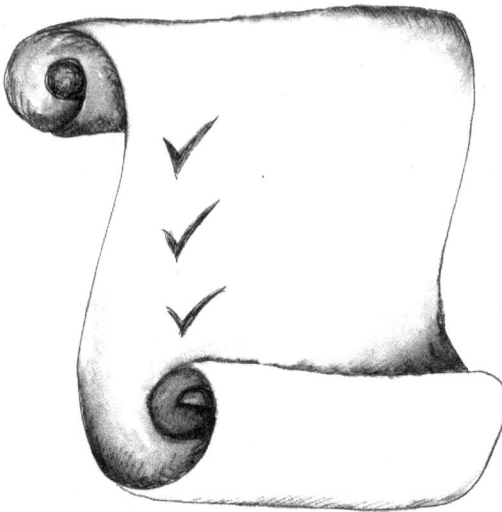

Figure 6.3 Accepting feedback with open arms tool

Inspiration

During my initial days of practice, I often found myself feeling more apprehensive during some therapeutic sessions than others. On trying to find the common thread for this repetitive feeling of discomfort, I found that these were most often clients who would express their unwillingness to be there, question my abilities or frequently express that whatever we were doing wasn't working for them. With a little more experience, I realised that what I was thinking of (rather catastrophically) as signs that I was forever doomed to fail at my occupation of choice was something a lot more useful to me – it was Feedback.

And feedback when used as an instrument can change the dynamics of the client-practitioner relationship to something truly collaborative instead of instructional or prescriptive. In fact, feedback can sometimes address the metaphorical 'elephant in the room', which once addressed may allow us more room for authentic interactions free from the many small regrets and resentments that can over time undermine the relationship between the individual and practitioner.

Feedback can come in verbal and non-verbal forms and in the forms of comments, questions, suggestions or complaints; so even after resolving to wholeheartedly accept and respond to feedback, questions may still remain as to how? The **'Accepting feedback with open arms'** *tool is a checklist that can be used to encourage, identify, classify and plan action in response to different kinds of feedback from an individual.*

Introduction

Feedback that we receive from someone we're working with is often a reflection of how the individual has been feeling in their past interactions with us. And depending on the sentiment and/or ideas that are reflected in these messages, we may choose to respond with slightly different nuances.

This tool helps classify feedback messages into a four-category checklist that may be used as a tool for screening for covert feedback as well as gain more insight into the ways in which feedback can take shape:

- Distrust Feedback
- Despair Feedback
- Difference Feedback
- Deference Feedback

1. DISTRUST FEEDBACK

Description	What it may look like	What to do
Doubts about the ability or intention	Many questions about practitioners' qualifications or the usefulness of the work Asking to contact someone with more seniority Ignoring the practitioner or agreed-upon plans of action Refusal to meet Withholding information	1 Gently enquire what the individual's current expectation or fear is about what may happen 2 Explain processes without defending their virtue 3 Highlight that they have choices that are at their disposal to make 4 Ask them what would be something they would choose to prioritise or are concerned may remain neglected while working together

Distrust Feedback refers to remarks, comments or behaviour that may convey that the individual doesn't yet fully trust you have the right intentions or skills to help them. When this seems to be a theme present in interactions with an individual, directly pointing out or refuting these assertions may be counterproductive and make an individual even more distrustful. It can be helpful over time to be as transparent about our ways of working together as possible, invite collaboration on setting small goals before moving on to larger goals, and have as consistent and non-reactive a disposition as possible.

2. DESPAIR FEEDBACK

Description	What it may look like	What to do
Hopelessness about the changeability of the current situation	Outbursts of sadness or fear Expressing feelings of being stuck Becoming silent or unresponsive when solutions are being discussed Direct communication of doubts with statements like 'nothing ever helps', 'I have already tried everything'	1 *Validate the person's feelings and the subjective distress that they may have been feeling for a long time* 2 *Encourage the individual to discuss what is the thing they would want a miracle to change* 3 *Working together, try to break this down into small bits that can be achievable* 4 *Start with the smallest and easiest task to set the person up with a feeling of mastery and success*

Sometimes when someone is dealing with a burden that they have been carrying for a long time or one that feels extremely overwhelming, they may express that they don't think it is possible or within anyone's ability to help them. This is **Despair Feedback**. When we receive such messaging from a person, it may be helpful to work with them into mapping out their problem into smaller bits, separating those that can be achieved in the short term and those that may take longer to tackle, discussing and brainstorming together on how each may be addressed.

3. DIFFERENCE FEEDBACK		
Description	**What it may look like**	**What to do**
Individual differences, neurodiversity and belongingness to specific socio-cultural identity groups	Direct disclosure of differences in ability, past diagnoses, identity group belongingness Often, information is available to the social worker or enquired during initial meetings but may come up in specific discussions more covertly	1 *Identify the difference that the individual is expressing and try to use open-ended questioning* 2 *Identify through questioning how this changes how they experience their problem* 3 *Discuss what boundaries and impediments this may include as well as what unique preferences or abilities the individual may wish to utilise* 4 *Discuss any past information or research you may have encountered that informs your practice and check if this information is accurate according to their lived experience*

Feedback of differences refers to when an individual gives feedback about their specific preferences, ways of working or circumstances that may catalyse our need to problem solve and work out a way to work with them most effectively. This sort of feedback is especially important to identify, address and act on with clients who may be neurodiverse and/or belong to underrepresented socio-economic, cultural and gender minorities. Often discussing directly what may be alternate ways of working together may be quite helpful. In some cases, we might also need to work on biases or beliefs that may have never been brought to awareness before. We need to be careful to not let our attachment to our identity as 'good people' or those with good intentions get in the way of us developing real-world insight into who we are and how we are received. And then adapt this information into an action plan that is most effective for who we are currently working with.

4. DEFERENCE FEEDBACK		
Description	**What it may look like**	**What to do**
Passive acquiescence to suggestions and interventions	Lack of input into conversations or talk sessions Expressions such as 'as you say' Lack of direct feedback or comments about what is being decided Rarely initiating discussions	1 *Structuring interactions in a way that leaves explicit space for their input in the plan of action* 2 *Highlighting our role as facilitator and not an authority figure* 3 *Present two or more choices on how to proceed to the next step and use open-ended questioning to increase the amount of input received*

Deference Feedback can refer to two slightly related types of feedback. As mentioned earlier, the dynamic of working with someone who comes with a problem that needs to be solved often creates a dynamic where the individual may assume the role of someone who listens and acquiesces to what the professional says. So, as practitioners it's very important to be aware of when someone seems to be agreeing to processes with remarks such as 'if you say so' or 'you probably know best'. Such remarks may indicate a need for us to provide explicit opportunities to the individual to tell us their own perception of the progress of our work together with what they think is working and what they think isn't working yet. Having check-ins after every meeting or every other meeting may be useful.

Theory

This tool draws from research that supports the assertions that integrating client feedback into psychotherapeutic practice can help improve therapy outcomes as well as research that demonstrated that positive alliances between client and practitioner improve treatment outcomes (Norcross and Lambert, 2018). Cognitive Behaviour Approaches emphasise the need to monitor and respond to feelings and affect as feedback. This forms the basis for this tool. Feedback can be verbal messages that denote a feeling and feelings expressed during an interaction are also a form of feedback.

When feedback is not verbal, it is advised that the practitioner directly check in on how the individual is feeling or what's going through their mind. Eliciting feedback about the quality of the session at its end is also suggested. This helps the process become collaborative. Feedback also helps clarify the individual's opinions about the practitioner, the techniques used and their expectations of the process (Beck, 2020). Ultimately receiving, acknowledging and acting on feedback helps strengthen the therapeutic alliance.

How to use the tool

To encourage more input from individuals, it may be helpful to ask more open-ended questions, check-in with their impression of progress at the end of sessions and introduce a new activity or technique within a session as a question so that it gives them an opportunity to comment and ask follow up questions about it. For example, 'Would you like to fill this form on your own?' rather than 'Okay please fill this form first'. In order to use this tool, the first step may be to at least in the beginning, keep note of any questions that an individual asks of you, or comments made about the session or interaction itself. Then, towards the end of the session, we examine these questions to see if we can observe any of the themes that have been mentioned in the tool. With practice we may be able to do this during the session as the feedback is being received. Then based on what type of feedback it is, we can try to follow the techniques to address them.

At the beginning of a session, the client remarked that they're not sure that us being there will actually be of any help. Here we could see that there was an element of Distrust Feedback. So, using the tool as a guide, we asked them what they expected was going to happen in our time together. She mentioned that she felt that she would be given a list of everything she had been doing wrong and asked to follow a new routine prescribed to her. Leading from this it was clarified that things might go a little differently as she would be the one helping us identify what the issue was and what worked best for her. Later, when suggesting that in order to introduce a mindfulness activity we may try meditation, the client remarks that they can't meditate sitting in one place as it makes them more restless and anxious. This is Difference Feedback. So we discuss when are the moments that the client feels least restless, the client remarks, 'well when I am already moving around!'. From this we arrive at that the client feels the most clear-headed when she is running as she is only able to focus on her breathing. Therefore, we are now able to come up with a way to achieve one of our goals while keeping in mind her unique preferences. In this way we use each of the items on our checklist to slowly address both resistance and concerns that arise in the course of an interaction between a practitioner and an individual.

Other ways to use the tool

The checklist may also find use by supervisors or practice educators to go over with students to better explore and monitor themes that come up during placement. The checklist could be used as a guide to reflective practice and monitor the way we are able to respond to feedback from those we work with at the end of sessions or while preparing to meet someone with lived experience for the first time. Conversely it can even be used to assess the way feedback is taken by the practice educator in the relationship with the learner to facilitate the theme of two-way learning in this dynamic.

Three key takeaway messages

1   Posing proposed actions as open-ended questions: This allows for most natural opportunities for the individual to add their own input to the interaction, comment and ask questions.
2   Identifying the underlying theme of the feedback: This mental categorisation helps create a starting point of accepting and analysing the feedback received.
3   Addressing the concern that the feedback raises using the tool: Once the broad nature of the feedback concern is identified, going through the steps to respond to it.

BUILDING THE FOUNDATIONS FOR A GOOD ENDINGS TOOL

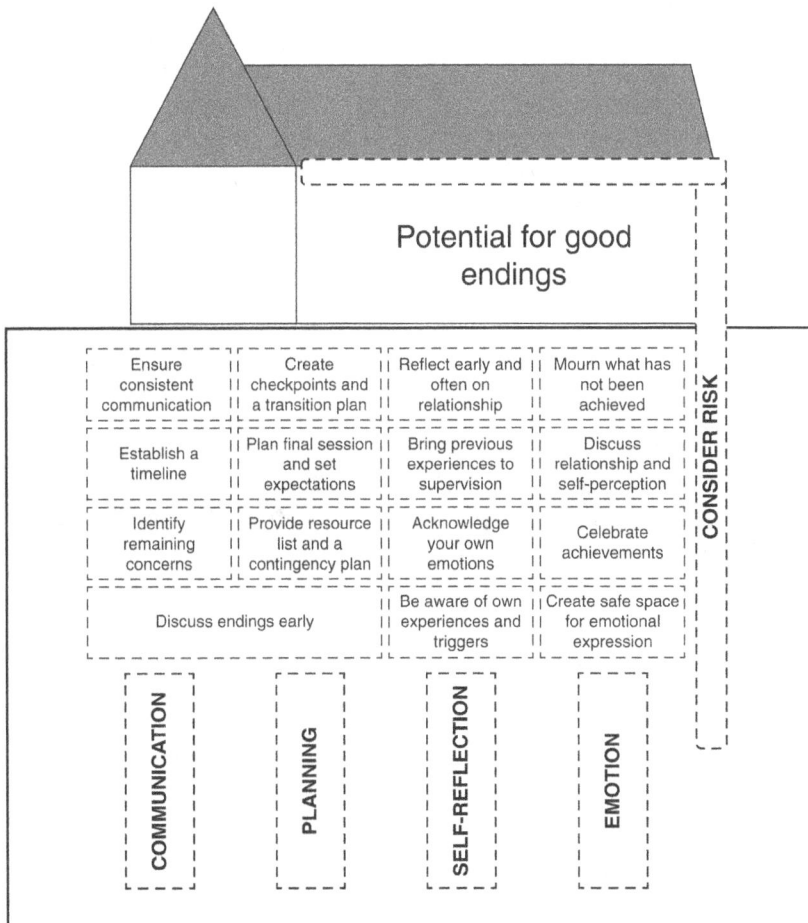

Figure 6.4 Building the foundations for a good endings tool

Inspiration

In my personal life, I have always found endings difficult. How to adequately acknowledge the impact that someone has had on my life, my gratitude and the sadness at no longer having that same relationship with them is something that I have really struggled with. I brought this to my professional work too. I quickly came to recognise how important endings were in therapy as this is something that is emphasised time and again in our training, but I worried whether I could provide those I worked with an adequate experience of endings. My aim was to craft endings in which we could recognise all that our work had achieved and mourn all that it had not. I was also concerned about whether I could provide an experience that would help someone to move forward once our work ceased. I hoped to create an environment where they felt able to openly express the range of feelings emanating from the ending. I started to realise that there were many different factors that could come together to form a good ending and that these had a way of complimenting and building on each other. Such structure and predictability are crucial particularly for those who have been through trauma, experienced instability or sudden changes in the past. I found that making the different aspects of endings explicit and visual aided me in thinking about how to provide the best possible experience for those I worked with.

Introduction

In social work it is important that an ending can be processed together with the individual, that their feelings can be heard and that the ending does not damage the relationship which has been developed with time and care. Endings are emotive and can frequently reignite previous experiences of other endings or losses. Endings are of such significance in therapy that in short-term therapy we work with the ending from the very beginning of the work. When an ending is conducted in a compassionate and skilful way, it can reinforce the work that has been undertaken and can empower the individual to move forward. If not given adequate thought and attention, then the progress that has been made may be lost and the client may be reluctant to engage with other practitioners in the future. This tool will help you to pinpoint some key areas to focus on when coming to the end of piece of work with an individual. Without this there is a risk that the person may experience feelings of abandonment, loss or anxiety about the end of the social work relationship. While not all endings can be predicted, there are still many other aspects that can be considered to make an ending as good as it can possibly be, even if it happens in less-than-ideal circumstances.

Theory

The concept of endings in therapy encompasses various theories and perspectives that address the termination phase. Beck's (2011) cognitive behavioural therapy approach involves planning for termination from the beginning of therapy. The focus is on equipping individuals with skills to maintain their progress independently. Bibring (1954) also emphasised the importance of endings, suggesting that if these are done well this allows those we work with to internalise therapeutic gains. Winnicott (1965) focused on the concept of 'good enough' endings, where the therapist provides a secure environment that enables someone to process separation and loss; this can be achieved by exploring the emotions around endings, whilst Perls (1969) placed the emphasis on completing unfinished business and achieving closure. Furthermore, Norcross (2011) emphasised the importance of tailoring the termination process to individual needs, incorporating elements from different therapeutic modalities to ensure a personalised and effective ending. In relational and intersubjective approaches, Benjamin (1988) focused on the co-constructed nature of the therapeutic relationship and the mutual recognition between the practitioner and the individual. In this approach the ending is seen as an opportunity to reflect on this relational dynamic. And finally, White (2007) viewed endings in narrative therapy as a continuation of someone's story. He placed the focus on empowerment and individuals continuing their journey beyond therapy.

How to use the tool

This tool (Figure 6.4) depicts the foundations on which good endings are built. At the very base there are four essential pillars – communication, planning, self-reflection and emotion – the building blocks laid on top of each of pillar relate to that topic. This tool is designed so that you can select the pillars that are most relevant to the specific ending with that individual. You can also select the most appropriate building blocks that sit on top of the relevant pillar. In this way the tool can be adapted to make it more person-centred; you can select the blocks that best fit with your work and also add in new pillars or blocks if needed. Enough blocks need to be present that there is a secure foundation on which a good ending can be built.

You also need to consider the risk present for any individual and whether this has been adequately managed. This is depicted by the drainpipe in the diagram. If the risk is not given due consideration, then it is possible that the drainage system might overflow and flood the foundations of the ending you have created, rendering them useless. For example, individuals may revert back to previous behaviours or may face set-backs as the relationship ends – this is why it is so important to ensure that the right resources and support networks are in place.

While most of the pillars might perhaps seem obvious, self-reflection may seem less so. Self-reflection is an essential part of the ending process; it enables practitioners to bring heightened awareness to their own responses, biases and assumptions, particularly in relation to trauma and other challenges clients may face. We will also often unconsciously repeat what has happened to us in terms of our own endings. This could manifest in different ways perhaps by trying to minimise or avoid the ending or by delaying these. Awareness of our own experiences around endings means we can engage more thoughtfully and intentionally in these and provide a better experience for those we work with.

As you work through the tool, highlight each building block and pillar as you incorporate it into your ending. By doing this you will have a visual representation of what you have put in place and also a reminder of any aspects that you may have overlooked. This tool can also be used collaboratively to plan the ending with an individual. It may help them visualise the steps around this, explore which aspects feel most important to them, providing them with greater autonomy and facilitating meaningful conversations. The tool could also be adapted based on an individual's age, developmental stage and communication needs and the language could be simplified if necessary.

I have been working with a client for a period of a year. Figure 6.5 shows how the tool would have been used with this client, I have highlighted the aspects that were relevant to this work.

In terms of planning: The ending of our work has been mapped out clearly from the beginning of our relationship and we have spoken repeatedly about this, including the end date. We also planned to meet less frequently as we approached then ending as part of our transition plan. We explored his support network when the sessions finished, and I provided him with a list of other resources he could access for support.

In terms of self-reflection: For my part, I found endings difficult in my work for the reasons I have discussed above. As a result, I felt guilty and uncomfortable in relation to this ending. Talking about this in supervision, I recognised that this reflected my own experiences of endings in relationships where perhaps I had not felt ready to say goodbye. Speaking about this helped me process my own feelings around the ending with this client, so that I did not unconsciously allow these to impact our work.

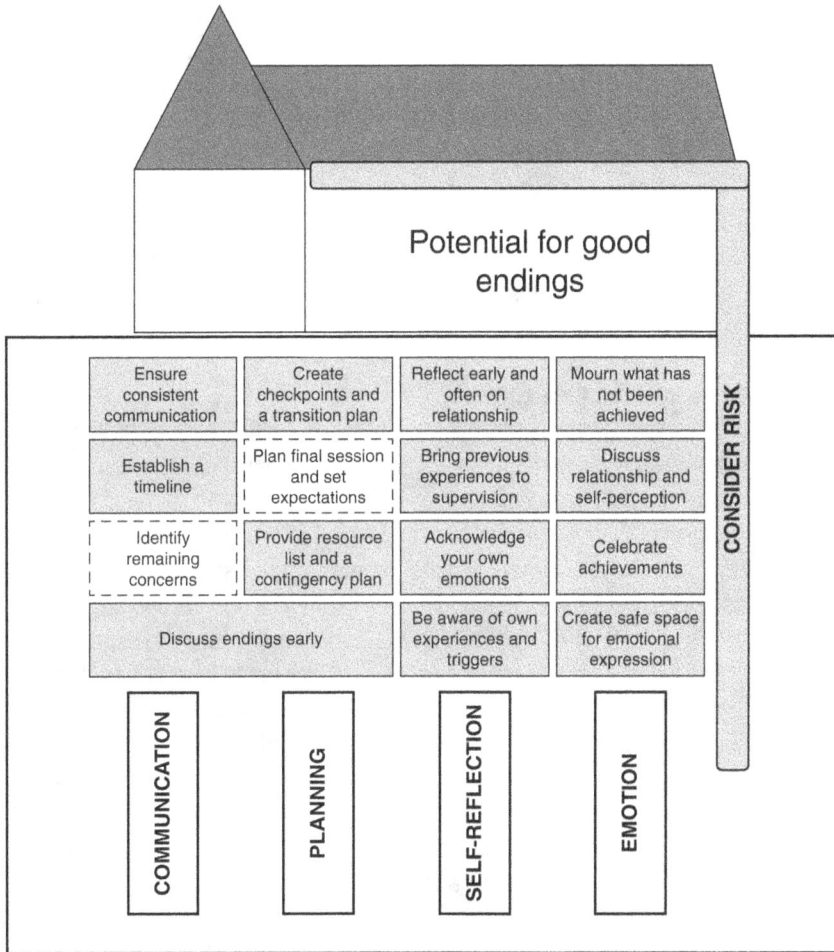

Figure 6.5 Potential for good endings

In terms of emotion: As we approached the final phase of our work, I would mention when we met, how many sessions were left and give him the opportunity to explore how he felt about this. As the work drew to close, we talked about our relationship and how he experienced this as well as how his perception of himself had changed during the work. We celebrated what has been achieved in our work and mourned what had not. He could see how far he had come but regretted that we did not have more time together. I viewed the fact that he was able to express this range of emotions openly as an achievement.

In terms of risk: He had a prior history of self-harm and addiction. We discussed this together and he felt he was in a good place to manage these at the ending of sessions. He was also aware of other places he could access support with these issues. He had a good relationship with his GP and was engaged in a 12-step program that he found extremely helpful. He confirmed that he felt able to access these resources after the conclusion of our work.

Through the work we undertook around this ending the client acknowledged that although he still found this painful, he felt more ready to face this than he otherwise would have.

Other ways to use the tool

The nature of being on placement may mean that students and apprentices have several endings in a short space of time as their work in a particular team comes to an end. Endings can be challenging for those new to practice who may be navigating many of these issues for the first time as a professional. Having a tool which helps them prepare for these endings can set them up from the beginning as practitioners capable of giving the individuals they work with good experiences of endings. This tool is useful as it helps to consider the many facets of endings early on and lays the groundwork for these from the beginning. Practice educators or onsite supervisors could use this tool to plan the ending of the placement with the student/apprentice. It can be used to explore which aspects might be most appropriate to each supervisee. Through this students and apprentices come to learn which aspects of endings are most important to them and thus it can facilitate their insight into themselves and give them an understanding of how it feels to experience this tool.

Three key takeaway messages

- **Personal Reflection and Emotions:** Reflect on your own experiences with endings and how they might influence your approach. Allow for exploration of your own experiences of endings in supervision. This will hopefully ensure that you can hear and respond to the full range of an individual's feelings about the ending.
- **Consistent Communication:** Maintain open and honest communication throughout the relationship. Ensure they are always informed about upcoming changes or the end of services.
- **Empower the Individual:** Encourage self-efficacy by reinforcing their strengths and abilities. Help them recognise their capacity to maintain progress independently.

REFERENCES

Beck, J.S. (2011) *Cognitive behaviour therapy: Basics and beyond*. 2nd edn. New York: Guilford Press.

Beck, J.S. (2020) *Cognitive behavior therapy: Basics and beyond*. 3rd edn. London, England: Guilford Press.

Benjamin, J. (1988) *The bonds of love: Psychoanalysis, feminism, and the problem of domination*. New York: Pantheon Books.

Bibring, E. (1954) 'Psychoanalysis and the dynamic psychotherapies', *Journal of the American Psychoanalytic Association*, 2(4), pp. 745–770.

Freud, S. (1900) *The interpretation of dreams*. 1st edn. New York: Macmillan.

Freud, S. (1913) *The interpretation of dreams*. 3rd edn. New York: Macmillan.

Norcross, J.C. (2011) *Psychotherapy relationships that work: Evidence-based responsiveness*. 2nd edn. New York: Oxford University Press, pp. 220–230.

Norcross, J.C. and Lambert, M.J. (2018) 'Psychotherapy relationships that work III', *Psychotherapy*, 55(4), pp. 303–315.

Perls, F.S. (1969) *Gestalt therapy verbatim*. Lafayette, CA: Real People Press, pp. 150–155.

White, M. (2007) *Maps of narrative practice*. New York: Norton & Company, pp. 220–230.

Winnicott, D.W. (1965) *The maturational processes and the facilitating environment: Studies in the theory of emotional development*. London: Hogarth Press.

Chapter 7

Coaching in social work to promote safety and well-being

Mark Dimes

INTRODUCTION

This chapter explores how coaching skills and techniques can be utilised to develop self-awareness and how the resulting coaching conversations can improve relationships and maintain and improve safety and well-being in social work practice. This will be achieved through the exploration of three interrelated tools with accompanying reflective activities, namely, **Values in Action (VIA)** to explore and reflect on individual character strengths, the use of the **GROW model** as a coaching framework in social work supervision and **SOLER** to better understand non-verbal communication and how this introspection can promote more meaningful conversations with people with lived or living experience, enhancing mutual trust and emboldening their social, emotional and mental well-being.

The tools are designed to assist with the smooth running and understanding of processes for each of the identified reflective activities with an explicit aim to enhance cognitive thinking and communication skills, essential to support the safety and well-being of all. We will look at how best to use these tools, ensuring that they become part of everyday thinking in social work practice. Coaching conversations, as a positive intervention, have the potential to assist individuals to develop solutions that promote mindset growth, increase confidence and help to understand what drives and motivates them.

For the social worker, this strength-based conversation focuses on the individual they are working with doing the talking, with the social worker asking questions that encourages the individual to explore their personal thoughts, feelings, hopes and goals. Coaching skills can easily be assimilated into social work practice; they promote personal insight, critical reflection and self-analysis, thereby nurturing best practice and the well-being of the people they are working with. In doing so, the anticipation is that social workers will improve their decision-making skills and

DOI: 10.4324/9781041054740-8

realign their thinking and behaviour, for example, in relation to the distribution of power in relationships. This will ensure that decisions and actions are non-coercive and self-determined, with people with lived experience's strengths and safety at the heart of practice.

Finally, we will provide key learning and summary points and consider other ways in which each tool could be accessed and utilised with individuals in social work practice. The rhetoric within local authority social work includes practitioners theoretically and practically being strengths-based, even though this approach can often be in direct contravention with the systems and processes in which they operate i.e. personal budget resource allocation system, which is a deficit-based model. As such, this chapter commits to using a strengths-based approach throughout and rather than using terms such as 'risk', the language focuses towards 'enhancing safety and wellbeing'. This approach is not denying the existence of a problem and instead, simply utilising a solution-focused, glass half-full mindset.

WHAT IS COACHING?

Coaching, in this context, is a two-way conversation designed to enable the person being coached, the coachee, time and space to explore their thoughts, feelings, behaviours and aspirations with the intention being for the coachee to clarify, understand and consider changes they wish to make in their life. In doing so, the assumed likelihood is that they will identify one or more solutions to a specific goal they have explored with the coach.

The role of the social work coach here is to facilitate conversations objectively, with minimal influence and judgement, echoing the words of Berg (2009) who declared that 'we should leave no footprints in our client's lives'. In this way, coaching is non-directive and non-judgemental, it's not for the coach to steer the coachee one way or another. The distance between solving someone's problem for them and helping them to solve their own problem can be quite broad. Therefore, a fundamental determination to be agreed upon by coach and coachee is how directive or non-directive the coach will be (Thompson, 2013).

The relationship is voluntary, i.e. the coachee chooses to be there, and therefore, by definition, this indicates a positive level of motivation and a commitment to change. Any change needs to be realistic; too large a goal between ideal and current behaviour may decrease confidence to change (Miller and Rollnick, 2002). The coach is not attempting to find the solution to the presenting issue; their role is to ask questions from which the coachee will elicit the answer they are looking for, an answer that they often already know without necessarily being fully aware of the possibilities. The voluntary nature of the relationship presents some consideration of the appropriate use of these tools across different fields of social work, where issues involving safeguarding or mental capacity may present more challenges. Nonetheless, key features of the tools such as the importance of intra-personal, non-verbal and observational skills utilised within the SOLER approach are applicable in statutory social work practice where there is a need to support positive change.

VALUES IN ACTION (VIA) – EXPLORING AND REFLECTING ON INDIVIDUAL CHARACTER STRENGTHS IN SOCIAL WORK SUPERVISION

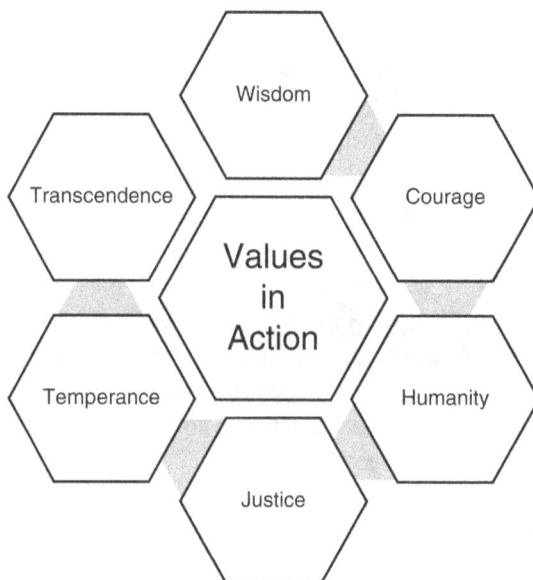

Figure 7.1 Values in Action (VIA) – exploring and reflecting on individual character strengths in social work supervision

Before we can hope to understand others, we must first gain insight to our own character and behaviour. What makes us tick and what might be some of the blind spots and areas for us to be mindful of? In this way, it is important to recognise that character strengths are relevant to every aspect of who we are as individuals, regardless of whether we are at work or at home.

Inspiration

VIA can be applied successfully to social work practice settings, for example, throughout conversations in social work supervision. Having completed the online tool and explored it themselves, supervisors (the coach) can introduce the tool to *new starters and learners (the coachee) during the early part of their induction and orientation to the workplace. The new starter should be given time to reflect on their survey results before sharing and exploring their individual character strengths in supervision. To help facilitate this conversation, the supervisor can utilise coaching questions to help the supervisee appreciate and understand their strengths.*

Pivotal to this notion is that social work centres on the dedication to serving and advocating for individuals, families and communities facing various challenges. The ability to engage in self-reflection and critical self-examination enables social workers to continually adapt and enhance their practice to address the diverse needs of those they support. This self-awareness is crucial as it directly influences decision-making processes and the quality of interventions. Without it, personal issues could unintentionally affect their professional judgement and effectiveness.

Introduction

The VIA (Values in Action) survey[1] is an online validated tool that can help individuals discover 'character strengths', including those that we tend to use and rely on the most (Peterson and Seligman, 2004). **VIA** identifies 24 positive character strengths which are reflected in our thoughts, feelings and behaviours. These strengths are categorised into six broad virtues (Ruch and Proyer, 2015):

Wisdom: Creativity, curiosity, judgement, love of learning, perspective.

Courage: Bravery, perseverance, honesty, zest.

Humanity: Love, kindness, social intelligence.

Justice: Teamwork, fairness, leadership.

Temperance: Forgiveness, humility, prudence, self-regulation.

Transcendence: Appreciation of beauty and excellence, gratitude, hope, humour, spirituality.

Copyright VIA

Theory

The **VIA tool** (Figure 7.1) can support individuals to recognise their personal strengths, confirming or perhaps contradicting previously held beliefs. The affirmation that follows can open the door to improved self-esteem and a more positive outlook on life, potentially enhancing emotional resilience and reducing negative beliefs we may have. It will also help to highlight the benefits of emotional recovery and personal growth with a rationale that identifies self-awareness as key to improving confidence and motivation, stimulating change talk, and positive movement towards safety and well-being goals. Solution-focused coaching, for example, can be utilised to help further identify these individual goals and aspirations (by using, for example, best hopes and scaling questions). And, by definition, this newfound personal insight can lead individuals to restore trust in themselves and to appreciate themselves more.

> *In the spring of 2023, I was working with a coachee who was finding it difficult to recognise their personal strengths, attributes that were quite apparent to me but were somehow not visible to the coachee. After discussing with a colleague, she told me about VIA, which is described on the VIA strengths website as a 'psychometrically validated personality test that measures an individual's character strengths'. And having completed the test myself and gained significant personal insight, I realised that this was an ideal tool to share with coachees, for them to complete before coaching or in between sessions for us to then explore further throughout our coaching conversations. After completing the test, the anticipation is that coachees have greater self-insight and awareness of their personal strengths, which in turn has the potential to promote a richer and more informed conversation during coaching. In a subsequent coaching session, the coachees declared that they had experienced a light bulb moment after completing VIA, such was the impact that they were genuinely excited about this insight into their own personality. It gave us the opportunity to discuss their top strengths in more detail, to explore the relevance and accuracy to them as an individual and how this could support their aspirations and best hopes moving forward.*

When applied in practice, these personal insights can help to improve self-belief and confidence, by raising awareness and highlighting strengths and attributes. Supervisors can encourage supervisees to envisage ways they can apply these strengths to current goals and situations in their daily life. Character strengths that lie further down the list offer us an opportunity for further learning and self-discovery and that's not about changing who you are but rather, identifying how you can improve your ability to build more personality insights leading to greater self-esteem and more meaningful relationships. In this way, increased self-awareness in social work fosters more empathetic and effective interactions and the process of developing self-awareness is essential for personal growth and improving lived experience outcomes. It is logical to assume, therefore, that ongoing personal insight and self-awareness will help to improve the ability to develop effective working relationships, augmenting decision-making and promoting more positive outcomes for people with lived experience.

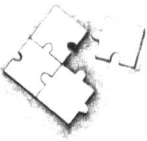

Particularly effective for new starters, learners and newly qualified social workers (NQSWs), this reflective activity can help to enhance self-awareness and will cultivate shared understanding, relational development and personal goals. Outcomes can be enhanced further if the supervisor has also completed and shared their test results with the supervisee.

- *Supervisee to complete the VIA survey after discussion in first supervision*
- *Supervisee reflects on test results – what have I learnt about myself and what difference will this insight mean to me and to others in my life?*
- *In their next supervision, both parties review the supervisee's top strengths and discuss how these have supported them in overcoming past challenges and explore any learning and insights identified through this exercise.*
- *Supervisor asks supervisee coaching questions (see Section 2 below for examples).*
- *Consider next steps, what needs to happen, what changes will I effect and how?*
- *Review character strengths periodically and connect with performance goals and annual appraisals.*
- *What else?*

There is little doubt that we can all reflect on past experiences and learn from them. Reflection helps us evaluate what worked, what could have gone better and how we can apply any lessons learnt to new situations. In turn, this will likely lead to further self-evaluation, potentially improving relationships, enhancing emotional regulation, allowing us to recognise when we need to adapt our strategies or behaviours to new circumstances. Furthermore, having increased self-awareness builds emotional resilience enabling us to better understand our coping mechanisms and stress responses (Hippe, 2004) and can also improve our ability to empathise with others (Younas *et al.*, 2020).

REFLECTIVE ACTIVITY

How might having greater insight into your character strengths promote individual's safety and well-being in your practice?

Think about your top character strength and consider what difference this insight will make to you and to others.

Change often triggers emotional responses such as anxiety or resistance. By being aware of these emotions, we can address them constructively rather than letting them hinder our progress, by developing strategies to stay resilient in the face of change. **VIA** can promote understanding of our strengths and limitations; it empowers us to set achievable goals during times of change, and with this realistic approach, we can hope to reduce the potential of frustration and burnout. Subsequently, within the confidential space offered by supervision, self-aware individuals are more likely to seek and accept feedback. This openness to feedback can help individuals adjust their strategies and behaviours to better navigate change and more effectively enhance safety in practice settings.

REFLECTIVE ACTIVITY

Now that you know your top strengths, what difference will that make to you and to others?

What else could you do to recognise any blind spots you might have?

The **VIA tool** can equally be applied in social work practice education, providing practice educators, onsite supervisors, and learners with a starting point for shared insights and mutual understanding. Developing self-awareness will benefit learners immeasurably during the early days of their social work career. And practice educators, in particular, will need to adopt a strengths-based, myth-busting approach, dispelling common assumptions, especially when supporting learners who may identify as being neurodivergent or culturally diverse.

It is logical to assume that the process of identifying and discussing thoughts, feelings and behaviours with the **VIA tool** will assist individuals to gain valuable insight into who they are and perhaps, through reflection, analysis and feedback, who they would like to be. And increased awareness and insight into personal blind spots will undoubtedly lead to more effective social work practice and support emotional resilience and enhance the well-being of social work learners (Grant, 2017).

SUMMARY

The VIA survey was developed by Peterson and Seligman (2004) based on values that are ubiquitous in all cultures and religions.

COACHING CONVERSATIONS IN SOCIAL WORK SUPERVISION USING THE GROW MODEL

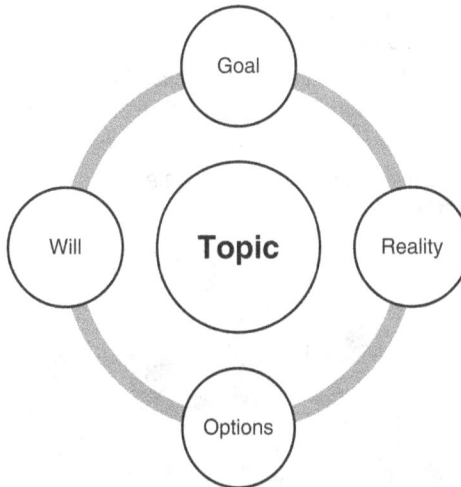

Figure 7.2 Coaching conversations in social work supervision using the GROW model

Introduction

The **GROW model**, originally constructed by Graham Alexander in the 1980s, is a flexible framework that can be applied in both professional and personal contexts. It's a powerful and practical coaching tool because it encourages a clear and structured approach to goal setting and solution finding, while also promoting active listening, self-reflection and personal growth.

Thompson (2013) describes the four areas explored through the mnemonic **GROW** as seen in Figure 7.2 and 7.3

Goal	What are you trying to achieve?
Reality	What is currently going on?
Options	What could you do?
Will	What will you do?

Inspiration

GROW *can be effectively applied to conversations with people with lived experience although Triggs (2023) identified that 'two very different mindsets were required to accommodate the difference in roles as a social worker and as a social work coach'. Perhaps the most obvious application of* **GROW** *in social work lies within the supervisory relationship. Broadly speaking, the purpose of supervision in this context is to facilitate good practice, protect members of the public and enable the professional development of supervisees.*

Non-managerial supervision linked to, for example, solution-focused coaching, 'gives centre stage to the skills, strengths, knowledge and experience of the (client) supervisee' (O'Connell and Palmer, 2007). Coaching, utilising **GROW***, validates the competence and resources of supervisees whilst emphasising the importance of self-awareness, critical reflection, clear outcomes and the need to focus upon*

Figure 7.3 Grow flowers

solutions rather than problems. In this way, good supervision raises skills levels, builds morale and improves motivation. The benefit of this approach is that it is a positive, affirming and confidence-building experience that engages supervisees in self-directed learning, focusing on outcomes, drawing upon what is working well, whilst generating innovative solutions.

The success of the **GROW model** is dependent on the supervisors' skills in asking questions that, through active listening, to promote supervisee personal insight and awareness. Working at their best, supervisors provide feedback and facilitate a conversation towards the development of a realistic and achievable action plan made by the supervisee. **GROW** encourages individuals to take ownership of their goals and decisions and can help to increase individual self-confidence and motivation.

GROW can be extended further, with the inclusion of T for Topic (especially when more than one goal has been identified) as a starting point and associated coaching cards, videos and sample questions are extensively available online.

G – GOALS – Think about goals as aspirations and desired destinations that the supervisee is hoping to move towards. The supervisor, utilising a solution-focused approach, will have no goal other than that formulated by the supervisee (Ratner, George and Iveson, 2012). The skill of the supervisor therefore centres on their ability to ask questions that will elicit insight and a clear description of the goals for the supervisee to explore further. It is an advantage if individuals can articulate clear goals, as it is more likely they will be achievable, and motivating. The SMART acronym (specific, measurable, achievable, relevant, and time-bound) can help to effectively establish these goals.

---

1   2   3   4   5   6   7   8   9   10

When someone describes their goals in terms of what they do not want, simply ask them, 'what do you want instead?'

---

1   2   3   4   5   6   7   8   9   10

'On a scale of 1 to 10'

R – REALITY – What is the current situation for the supervisee in relation to their identified goal? Scaling can help to consider what has happened so far to reach it. This part of the conversation will involve the supervisor asking clarifying questions and checking out assumptions, exploring any challenges, and identifying progress already made by the supervisee (O'Connell, 2012).

An agreed-open and honest representation of the present situation is essential for the supervisee to move forward with their well-defined goal and the strategic options needed to achieve it. The supervisor is inviting the supervisee to delve deeper, fostering an environment that invites frank dialogue, reflection and introspection on the part of the supervisee. It is anticipated that this process will reveal traits that stimulate and enhance well-being, self-care and mindfulness.

O – OPTIONS – We now need to encourage the supervisee to explore the options open to them and it is important to be open-minded about this action as it's likely that more creative options will come to the fore, encouraging the supervisee to consider potential strategies to reach the goal they have identified. The anticipation is that this process of cognition will raise awareness and highlight areas of risk associated with people with lived experience's safety and well-being.

---

1 2 3 4 5 6 7 8 9 10

'On a scale of 1 to 10 with ten representing the best it can be and one the worst where would you say you are today?'

'What would need to happen for you to move up the scale?'

What have you learned from other times in your life that would be useful to you now?

W – WILLPOWER – The final phase can also be viewed as the 'Way Forward' and involves the supervisee committing to concrete actions, establishing specific steps they will take to reach their goal, and may also explore potential obstacles and ways to overcome them. Motivation and confidence to succeed is key here, and once more scaling techniques can be employed to establish how the supervisee will know they have been successful.

The 'Will' phase represents the propulsion that drives the supervisee from their current reality towards their desired aspirations. It's here where a commitment to action is forged and a realistic plan is developed. As we have witnessed with VIA above, critical to this process is an understanding of strengths (and limitations) as this will enable individuals to set achievable SMART goals during times of change and this realistic approach is therefore more likely to reduce the potential of frustration and burnout.

Theory

The GROW model is based on several key theories and principles from psychology and management:

> **Goal Setting Theory:** Developed by Edwin Locke and Gary Latham (1984), this theory emphasises the importance of setting specific, challenging and attainable goals to enhance performance. The **GROW model's** first step, 'Goal', aligns with this theory by encouraging clear and measurable objectives. Setting clear goals, aligned to organisational objectives, is essential for effective risk and safety management. Regular reviewing and monitoring of goals will help to address any emerging risks or changes in the environment.

> **Reality Therapy:** Created by William Glasser (2012), this approach focuses on the present and encourages individuals to evaluate their current behaviour and its effectiveness in meeting their needs. The 'Reality' step in the **GROW model** reflects this by assessing the current situation and identifying obstacles.

> **Options Theory:** This theory involves exploring various strategies and solutions to achieve goals. It is rooted in decision-making theories that emphasise the importance of considering multiple alternatives before making a choice. The 'Options' step in the **GROW model** is about brainstorming and evaluating different paths.

> **Action Planning:** Derived from project management and behavioural psychology, this principle emphasises the need for a clear plan of action to achieve goals. The 'Way forward' step in the **GROW model** involves creating a detailed action plan, assigning responsibilities, and setting timelines.

These theories collectively provide a robust framework for the **GROW model,** making it an effective tool for coaching and personal development in social work.

In supervision, Tony talks to his supervisor about an individual who is 74 years of age and lives alone, and who has recently experienced psychological and financial abuse. Tony is anxious about this situation and is struggling to move forward as he explores and seeks out solutions to the person with lived experience's predicament. With mental capacity assured and the individual remaining vulnerable to abuse, during supervision,

Tony's supervisor utilises the GROW model with Tony, allowing him time to work through his anxieties and contemplate any identified goals, consider the reality and ponder the options open to him as a social worker (acknowledging that the approach can only be successfully applied to ourselves and not to a third party). Tony determines that the individual is fully aware of the situation and the choices they have, and he is clear that he has explored all available options and possible solutions with them. The GROW model has helped to inform and validate Tony's professional opinion, and he acknowledges that he has done what he can to support the individual, for now at least. The clarity provided through this process has given Tony some self-belief and confidence and has reassured him that developing an action plan with the individual before ending his involvement will be a satisfactory way forward.

*Applying the **GROW model** in supervision will likely lead to supervisees achieving specific goals, but it also fosters a supportive and developmental relationship between supervisor and supervisee and encourages continuous learning and professional growth. Figure 7.4 describes the suggested flow of any conversation within supervision. However, the model should be used flexibly, largely because, for example, establishing the goal may require a discussion about the reality and/ or the options before being fully able to identify and define the goal. In this way, **GROW** should not be seen as a linear process as the movement around and interplay between the different stages are integral to its success.*

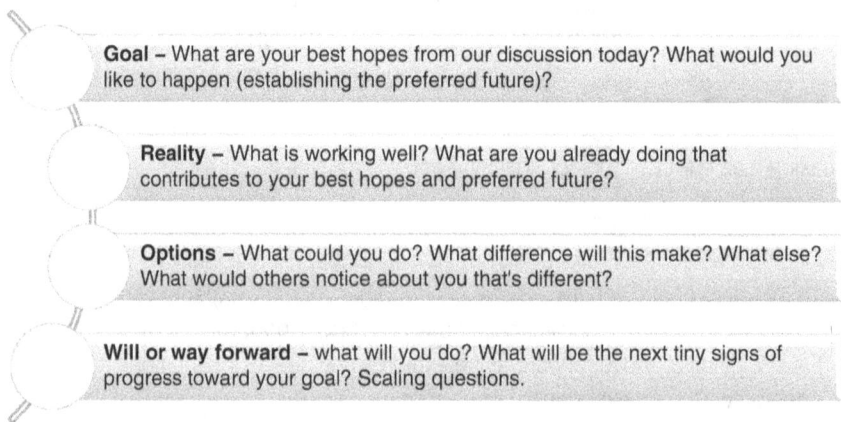

Goal – What are your best hopes from our discussion today? What would you like to happen (establishing the preferred future)?

Reality – What is working well? What are you already doing that contributes to your best hopes and preferred future?

Options – What could you do? What difference will this make? What else? What would others notice about you that's different?

Will or way forward – what will you do? What will be the next tiny signs of progress toward your goal? Scaling questions.

Figure 7.4 GROW model

How to use the tool

The **GROW model** complements solution-focused coaching techniques, for example, through future-focused open-ended questions and the identifying of exceptions to the presenting scenario (e.g. times when the supervisee has successfully coped with or addressed previous difficulties that support the identified GOAL).

REFLECTIVE ACTIVITY

Think about and reflect on a specific goal you would like to discuss in supervision.

What will be your best hopes from this discussion?

Summarising by the supervisor is key to help clarify understanding, as is the notion of reframing any deficit language used by the supervisee. For example, supervisees stating that they 'don't want to feel stressed' might lead the supervisor to respond with 'what would you like to feel instead?' Using questions such as 'what else?', 'what difference would that make?' and 'what would others notice about you?' are beneficial to assist both parties to understand the GOAL and subsequent description of the REALITY.

On a scale of 1–10, how confident are you that you will be able to meet your identified GOAL?

What difference will this make to you?

What will others notice about you that's different?

What else?

Supervisors will benefit from being comfortable with silence, allowing supervisees time to think and consider their OPTIONS, standing back and avoiding the temptation to provide answers. Once more, 'what else?' questions by the supervisor continue to ask the supervisee to delve deeper to explore previously unthought ideas, solutions and potential ways forward. Scaling questions fit nicely when looking to identify confidence levels, motivation and the coachees WILL do change, do something different, and commit to action.

Throughout these conversations, it's important for both parties to consider power and power dynamics in their relationship. Power dynamics can be described as the way in which different people interact, often where one of these sides is more powerful than the other. In social science and politics, it is the ability to influence (or even control) the behaviour of people. Power dynamics can and do affect relationships and a balanced relationship, where power is held equally, may occur where both parties listen to each other and make changes based on the feelings and interests of the other. They respect each other, even in times of disagreement and they talk to each other, especially when issues develop.

SOLER: EFFECTIVE VERBAL AND NON-VERBAL COMMUNICATION IN SOCIAL WORK PRACTICE

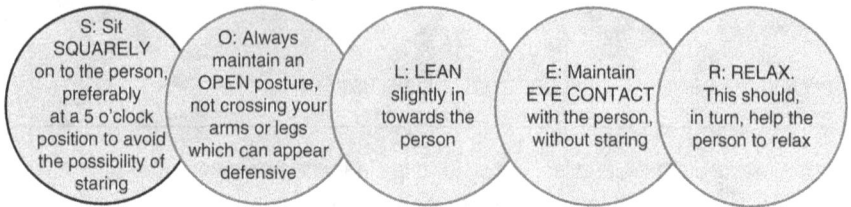

S: Sit SQUARELY on to the person, preferably at a 5 o'clock position to avoid the possibility of staring

O: Always maintain an **OPEN** posture, not crossing your arms or legs which can appear defensive

L: LEAN slightly in towards the person

E: Maintain EYE CONTACT with the person, without staring

R: RELAX. This should, in turn, help the person to relax

Figure 7.5 SOLER: effective verbal and non-verbal communication in social work practice

Inspiration

The relevance and importance of **SOLER** *is that, through discussion, feedback, observation and reflection (in supervision for example), it can help to improve self-awareness, and intra-personal skills that critically influence the ability to develop rapport and understanding. It's argued that with this personal insight, you are more likely to foster effective working relationships with members of the public, supporting individuals to incrementally move towards a life that is safer and more secure. Adopting a* **SOLER** *mindset in practice is particularly useful when undertaking community visits, for example, into people's homes with its simplicity being its strength. Greater insight to individual living circumstances and a better understanding of the person you are visiting will almost certainly boost the effectiveness of any intervention with the anticipation that safe solutions to presenting problems can be found.*

Introduction

Gerad Egan (1990) developed **SOLER**, and it is a key component of his 'Skilled Helper' approach to counselling, which can be easily applied to social work practice, as both approaches focus on non-verbal communication and active listening, which are crucial for effective interpersonal interactions, rapport building and relational development. **SOLER** is an acronym (Figure 7.5) that is used to summarise this process and is a helpful tool for us to analyse our non-verbal interactions.

Figure 7.6 Drawing of two people sat on chairs

When observing a student visiting a person with lived experience in their home for the first time, I noticed that the student chose to sit on the sofa next to the individual and was thereby unable to maintain sufficient eye contact with them. She spoke fast and softly, not checking that what she had said had been heard and understood. She then became visibly impatient when the person asked her to repeat what had been said. I struggled to hear her as well, and when she repeated herself, it seemed that she was irritated by having to restate what she appeared to believe she had already made clear and apparent. The visit concluded with little progress being made and I observed that vital information may have been missed. In the car, on the way back to the office, I asked the student to reflect and talk to me about her thoughts and feelings from the visit. She told me that she had felt nervous and didn't know where to sit and that maybe, in hindsight, sitting opposite the person may have elicited a more productive and insightful conversation. It was clear at that point that we had both learnt from this experience as key to its success would have been a discussion on **SOLER**, in supervision, before the home visit had taken place (Figure 7.6).

Theory

The example above highlights the absence of insight to **SOLER** by a student social worker as well as the benefit of preparation and discussion in supervision, for example, before venturing out into community settings. The apparent basic understanding of where to position yourself in proximity to the person you are talking to should not be assumed. A discussion on the **SOLER** model before application in practice will undoubtedly improve outcomes, ensure that vital information to support the safety and well-being of all is not overlooked, and enable learners to build enhanced rapport and trust, making it easier for people with lived experience to share their thoughts, feelings and aspirations.

SOLER is a valuable tool for anyone in a helping profession, enhancing the effectiveness of their interactions, not least because non-verbal communication is underpinned by several key theories and principles from psychology and communication studies. These include **proxemics** (examining the use of space in communication), **kinesics** (focusing on body movements, gestures and facial expressions as forms of communication and emphasises that body language can convey a wide range of emotions and intentions), **paralanguage** (related to vocal elements that accompany speech, such as tone, pitch and volume), **chronemics** (exploring how the timing of interactions, punctuality and the pace of speech can influence communication dynamics) and **Facial Action Coding System** (FACS) (understanding how facial expressions correlate with specific emotions).

> *When I undertook the social work practice education qualification many years ago, one of the assignments focused on self-directed, experiential learning (see Knowles, 1978). This involved video recording of a supervision session with a student, with a specific remit for me to reflect and write about what I observed of myself in practice. And I was genuinely surprised at what I saw, seated as I was at right angles to the student, with a desk between us, six feet apart, with minimal eye contact. I noticed that I was distracted by playing with my pen and writing notes, and at one point the student explained a scenario and asked me a question. Somewhat incredulously, I moved on to talk about something else, hardly acknowledging what had been said. Recalling this event, I can't help but think that our relationship, that my focus and attention would have been greatly enhanced if I had applied the principles of **SOLER** to my practice?*

How to use the tool

Direct and indirect compliments based on careful observation of positive things that people have done or said are an essential part of relationship development and should be used throughout social work practice. Being curious and validating what people are already doing well and acknowledging how difficult their problems are encourages them to change and can enhance well-being, while giving the message that the social worker has been listening (i.e. understands) and cares. The trusting relationship that will emerge from this practice is likely to promote conversations that broaden and deepen shared understanding, providing a richer and more detailed description of current circumstances, thoughts, feelings, hopes and fears. It is hoped that armed with this newfound information, the social worker will be better placed to recognise and ameliorate risk factors and safety concerns.

When applying the **SOLER** model in practice, it is important to be mindful of some common mistakes that can undermine its effectiveness. For example, while maintaining eye contact is crucial, staring too intensely could make the person feel uncomfortable or intimidated and leaning too far forward could invade personal space. It is also beneficial to present as being relaxed, too rigid in posture can come across as unnatural or tense and consistency with this approach can help to build trust and rapport.

REFLECTIVE ACTIVITY

In conversation, observe how you and others use your hands and arms to communicate.

Is this helpful or just a distraction and will this insight change what you do?

What else do you notice and what difference will any changes make?

Social workers need to be mindful of potential cultural differences as we all have varying norms for body language and eye contact and remember, **SOLER** as a model is a guideline, not a strict rule. Try to adapt your body language to the context and the person's level of comfort and in doing so, consider any reasonable adjustments that might be helpful to the individual (for example, due to poor eyesight or hearing loss).

Extending beyond **SOLER**, we can observe that the pace, tone, language and pitch of what we say can all impact the quality of conversation (Figure 7.7). The pace of a conversation can inhibit effective communication, as speaking too quickly can make it hard for listeners to follow, while speaking too slowly can lose their interest. Adjusting your pace to the individual can help you to emphasise important points and maintain engagement. And your tone indicates the emotional quality of your voice, conveying your attitude and feelings, and a warm enthusiastic tone, is more likely to draw people into what's being said.

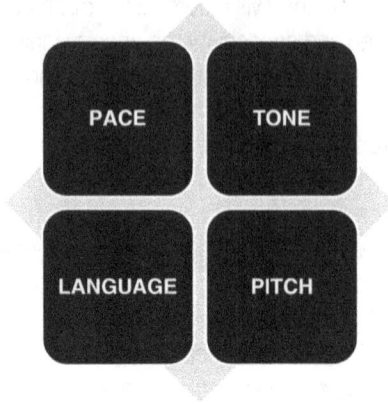

Figure 7.7 Pace – tone – language – pitch

Language is key to effective communication, relating to the choice of words and how they are structured.

Avoiding acronyms, jargon and complex words by using clear, concise and appropriate language ensures that your message is understood and will make your communication more accessible to others. Pitch relates to the highness or lowness of your voice and varying your pitch can convey different emotions. For example, a higher pitch can indicate excitement or urgency, while a lower pitch can convey calmness or authority.

SOLER is an effective model that can be introduced to the practice learning environment, extensively through supervision, observation in practice and critical reflection. The examples provided highlight that we should not assume that everybody understands the important elements and detail of non-verbal communication. One of the keys to this will be for practice educators to explain and model best practice, perhaps by noticing and describing to the learner, incongruities that stand out. For instance, when someone makes a repetitive or distinctive gesture, a notable facial expression or significant change in voice tone or pitch.

REFLECTIVE ACTIVITY

Consider how you could relate to someone if you were seated back-to-back. You couldn't see their face, their body, their movements and expressions.

What difference would that make to you and to them?

Three key learning points

1   A critical aspect of intra-personal skills development centres on the journey of self-discovery, identity and awareness of individual character strengths. Navigating thoughts, feelings, opinions and perspectives will undoubtedly open doors and I've witnessed many 'lightbulb' moments of realisation in others through this insight. By understanding and managing our own thoughts and emotions, we can more effectively empower individuals we work alongside, and this will assist with the advancement of more trusting relationships to support the safety and well-being of all. In this way, and with the important addition of recognising your cultural lens and being sensitive to different worldviews, you will enhance trust and foster mutual respect with the people you are working with. In this way, expediting change talk towards safety goals with people with lived experience can be best achieved by first understanding yourself. In this context, the role of the supervisor is to help facilitate this journey, not by plotting a course or deciding the destination, but merely by standing at the helm.

2   Coaching conversations utilising the **GROW model**, can help to reduce assumptions and power imbalances, shifting the focus to, for example, what the supervisee wants to achieve rather than what the supervisor desires of them. They add structure whilst encouraging self-determination, empowering individuals to identify their own solutions to move forwards. Understanding what the person wants to achieve is the first step towards knowing what needs to happen for people to feel safe and supported. The next time someone is talking to you about an issue they have, consider listening to them and ask questions using the four areas of the **GROW** mnemonic.

3   Applying **SOLER** in your social work practice will help you to create more effective working relationships with individuals and their carers, enhancing effective communication and building stronger trust and connection. This will be a platform to enable people to make more informed decisions, that will hopefully empower and shield them better from future adversity and promote the safety and well-being of all. Remember, using common everyday language tells people that they can speak to us, and we can understand each other. The fundamentals in social work are by far the most effective, and practice makes perfect so don't be afraid to regularly observe yourself, analyse your behaviour, be curious and reflect on this further, seeking feedback as you go.

NOTES

1   https://www.viacharacter.org/

REFERENCES

Berg, I.K. (2009) 'Assessment and evaluation', *Solution-Focused Substance Abuse Treatment*, 71.

Egan, G. (1990) *The skilled helper: A systematic approach to effective helping*. 4th edn. Monterey, California: Thomson Brooks/Cole Publishing Co, pp. 71–92.

Glasser, W. (2012) *Reality therapy: A new approach to psychiatry*. New York: Harper Collins.

Grant, L. (2017) 'Enhancing resilience and wellbeing in social work: A toolbox approach', in *Paper presented at the BASW Annual England Conference & Annual Meeting 2017: Celebrating Success – We Have the Knowledge*, Leicester.

Hippe, J. (2004) '*Self-awareness: A precursor to resiliency*', *The Journal Reclaiming Children and Youth: The Journal of Strength-Based Interventions*, 12(4), p. 240.

Knowles, M. (1978) *The adult learner: A neglected species*. Houston, Texas: Gulf.

Locke, E. and Latham, G. (1984) *Goal setting: A motivational technique that works*. New Jersey: Prentice Hall.

Miller, W.R. and Rollnick, S. (2002) *Motivational interviewing: Preparing people for change*. 2nd edn. New York: Guilford Press.

O'Connell, B. (2012) *Solution-focused therapy*. 3rd edn. London: Sage.

O'Connell, B. and Palmer, S. (2007) *Solution-focused coaching*. London: Routledge.

Peterson, C. and Seligman, M. (2004) *Character strengths and virtues*. Washington: American Psychological Association and New York: Oxford University Press.

Ratner, H., George, E. and Iveson, C. (2012) *Solution focused brief therapy, 100 key points and techniques*. Oxford: Routledge, Taylor & Francis.

Ruch, W. and Proyer, R. (2015) '*Mapping strengths into virtues: The relation of the 24 VIA-strengths to six ubiquitous virtues*', *Frontiers in Psychology*, 6, pp. 1–12.

Thompson, B. (2013). *Non-directive coaching, attitudes, approaches and applications*. St Albans: Critical Publishing, p. 3.

Triggs, S. (2023) '*Becoming a 'social work coach': How practising coaching creates beneficial agility in social work identity*', *British Journal of Social Work*, 54, pp. 1–19.

Younas, A., Rasheed, S.P., Sundus, A. and Inayat, S. (2020) '*Nurses' perspectives of self-awareness in nursing practice: A descriptive qualitative study*', *Nursing & Health Sciences*, 22(2), pp. 398–405.

Chapter 8

Using IDEAS to support relational social work practice when working with risk

Heidi Dix

INTRODUCTION

Meaningful relationships are the bedrock of social work practice. They are created using the knowledge, understanding and skills to build and sustain relationships underpinned by professional values. In recent years there has been a growing recognition of the importance of re-emphasising relationship-based practice in social work such as the British Association of Social Work's 80-20 Campaign (British Association of Social Workers (BASW), 2018) which drew attention to child and family social workers' time being split between 80% administration work and 20% direct work contact. The importance of relational practice within adult social work practice was strengthened within the Care Act (2014) which placed the need for meaningful relationships at the heart of interactions between people who use services as well as between practitioners.

Whilst there is not a widely accepted definition of relationship-based practice, what most descriptions have in common is the idea that the ability to develop and sustain relationships with adults and children is key to achieving positive outcomes (Dix, Hollinrake and Meade, 2019; Howe, 1998; Megele, 2015; Munro, 2011; Trevithick, 2014). This chapter will describe the **IDEAS framework** which outlines a set of interconnected knowledge, skills, attitudes and personal qualities that evidence suggests are necessary to be an effective, relational practitioner in the human services and provides two other tools, **the IDEAS approach to anti-racist practice** and **using IDEAS to support defensible decision making**. The chapter also provides suggestions for developing a culture of effective practice within organisations where practitioners feel supported and psychologically 'contained' (Ruch, 2009) in their work which is becoming ever more complex and challenging.

DOI: 10.4324/9781041054740-9

EVIDENCE-INFORMED PRACTICE AND THE IDEAS FRAMEWORK

Evidence-informed social work practice draws on a range of knowledge from formal and informal sources. This can be through

- The lived experiences of carers and users of services.
- Research knowledge generated by academics and via co-production.
- Policy knowledge applied through national and local guidance.
- Organisational knowledge gathered by those responsible for the provision of services. This is usually obtained through management systems, quality assurance processes and oversight mechanisms.
- Practitioner knowledge often referred to as practice wisdom or 'stuff we just know' which comes from experience and is further developed by reflective practice.

Introduction

The **IDEAS** framework is an acronym which draws on the above sources of knowledge to describe the balance between the different aspects of social work practice that evidence suggests are necessary to be effective and can help practitioners to evaluate their relational practice. The key themes from existing sources of knowledge were pulled together into five separate although interlinked parts, called *Influence*, *Delivery*, *Expertise*, *Alliance* and *Support* which are outlined in more detail below. The human body will be used to illustrate how the different components of **IDEAS** need to be considered as a whole framework to help practitioners to reflect upon their practice and identify strengths and areas of development.

Inspiration

My colleague Jen and I were working in a youth justice setting and were curious about how best to support children and their parents and carers who are in contact with the youth justice system. At the time there was a strong emphasis on evidence-informed programmes as interventions and we both came from social work with adults backgrounds and were passionate about the importance of relational practice which seemed to be a missing component in the policy and practice guidance that was then available to us. To help us to gain an understanding of the skills, knowledge and values that were required, we reviewed the evidence available at the time and pulled together the key themes to form **IDEAS**. *Although* **IDEAS** *originated in the specialism of youth justice, the framework can be used as a quality assurance and reflective tool within most if not all areas of social work.*

TOOL 1: IDEAS FRAMEWORK FOR EFFECTIVE SOCIAL WORK PRACTICE

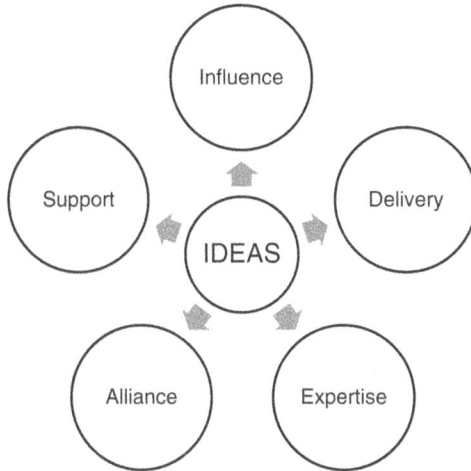

Figure 8.1 Tool 1: IDEAS framework for effective social work practice

Influence

Influence is the first element of the **IDEAS** framework (Figure 8.1) and is basically about being influential in a positive way. It is the element of **IDEAS** which is connected to the use of authority and power in a way which is value based and considers the conscious use of authority in the social work role (often referred to as legitimate authority) and so influence involves an understanding of anti-discriminatory, anti-oppressive and anti-racist practice. Influence is acknowledging that although as a worker we may share some characteristics with the people we work with, such as the same gender, or ethnicity, and these similarities can help the development of an effective relationship, it is also about being clear that power differentials exist and therefore understanding the privileges we may have and being open and transparent about these, to create a trusting relationship.

Influence describes the importance of practitioners understanding their role, the boundaries and limitations within it as well as the statutory aspects to consider how we can use this influence effectively. Often working with other services and agencies is an important part of social work practice and so Influence can also be considered to include an aspect of advocacy and the ability to positively influence others through skills and behaviours. It involves recognising and working with the fact that in many statutory settings the worker will usually have the authority to make decisions that can have consequences, such as detaining people, arresting people and the allocation of resources. Influence involves not just recognising this but being fair and consistent and therefore is about considering power and using it appropriately to effect positive change.

An example of influence in practice is that if we are working with a person with learning disabilities, we may need to influence interventions and support the care sector to tailor their services to accommodate the wide diversity of need presented by people with learning disabilities to ensure a personalised approach based on participation in community resources. We also need to use the legitimate authority in our role to actively challenge and advocate for people we are working with calling out discrimination and oppression and actively disrupting this.

Examples of theory that underpins this element

- Social learning theory (Bandura, 1971)
- Pro-social modelling and use of legitimate authority (Rex and Maltravers, 1998)
- French and Raven's five bases of power (1959)
- Empowerment theory (Rappaport, 1981)
- Models of anti-discriminatory and anti-oppressive practice such as Thompson's Personal, Cultural and Societal (PCS) model (2021), and Tedam's 4D2P framework (2021).
- Critical Race Theory (Bell, 2007)

We sometimes use the analogy of the human body as a way of illustrating the model, as although each element is distinct, they are all vital and need to work together. So, Influence is illustrated as the blood supply (Figure 8.2) which connects all the other elements and is essential to their functioning but often works in the background behind the scenes.

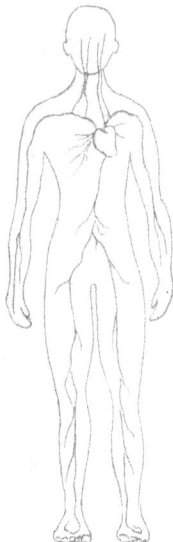

Figure 8.2 The blood supply as influence

Delivery

This element of the framework stands for the consideration of the professional tools and systems that support practice, such as assessment and the ability to apply them skilfully within organisational frameworks and processes. It includes practicing within agency policies and procedures to determine need and assess risk and safety, and then undertaking collaborative planning and intervention processes, all of which are determined by legislation, political ideology and organisational priorities. It also encompasses the need to adhere to professional expectations as set out by BASW's Professional Capabilities Framework (PCF) and the Social Work England Standards.

Legal literacy is complimentary to relationship-based practice because a good working knowledge of the legal framework supports the practitioner's ability to be transparent, honest and open about expectations, rights and needs. Delivery is about the skilful use of the relevant practice framework, for example, working within

- Policies and procedures (including safeguarding policies and procedures);
- Standards and professional boundaries;
- Using the approved assessment tools and keeping to timescales.

Practitioners who are skilled in this aspect of their work recognise that accurate and timely assessment, planning and record keeping are an essential part of effective practice not an 'add on' or a distraction from the 'real work'. Recording and filling in case records is not the most popular aspect of our work, nevertheless, Delivery is about transparency and accountability, not just to the agency but to people we are working with, and provides an important safety net for practitioners and those working with them.

If influence is about the appropriate and mindful use of authority (personal and professional), then delivery is about the way in which that authority is put into practice to ensure an effective service, through a co-productive and participatory relationship-based approach.

D can also stand for dominance linked to managerialist and bureaucratic processes such as key performance indicators and rigid eligibility criteria, so you would not wish to overemphasise the importance of this element and not consider the importance of personal and professional power and the time required to develop a positive relationship.

This element is described as the skeleton as it provides the framework for practice (Figure 8.3).

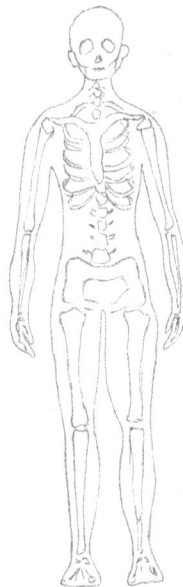

Figure 8.3 The skeleton as the framework for practice

Expertise

The E stands for expertise and refers to the knowledge, theory and research that informs practice and underpins skills relating to the practitioner's specific field of practice, such as adult and community social work, youth justice, child and family social work or knowledge in relation to domestic abuse. Practitioners need to know and understand the existing evidence base about what is effective in the particular area and the importance of keeping up to date with new developments. They will need to draw on critical thinking skills to enable them to assess the evidence of a particular approach or method in any given setting. They also require practice wisdom, that is the learning which comes from experience combined with the process of critical reflection, either individually or within supervision.

It also involves drawing on what experts by experience tell us is necessary.

Practitioners often say they value the ability to be creative in their work and having knowledge of research and evidence that works helps this. Expertise is the element which has to be present to allow creativity to flourish as it ensures that innovative ways of working are grounded in a foundation of a wide range of knowledge.

For obvious reasons, this element of the framework is referred to as the mind (Figure 8.4).

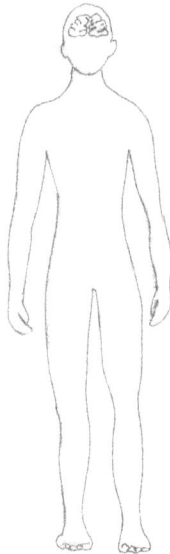

Figure 8.4 The mind as expertise

Alliance

This is the ability to develop trusting relationships with people with lived experience. This is particularly necessary when working with children and adults who may have a fear of authority for several reasons. Empathy, respect, warmth, integrity, transparency and trust are the foundations of an effective working relationship. Consistently research suggests that being persistent and hopeful can help people to develop a belief in a possible and positive future which can lead to change taking place. Whilst establishing a working relationship is important, it is not sufficient in isolation and a sense of purpose and focus on collaborative outcomes and a clear sense of direction that makes sense to the service participant through a co-productive approach is necessary.

'Tuning-in' (Taylor and Devine, 1993) and offering an empathic response, without judgement, whilst not colluding, can help people feel listened to and validated, all important factors to help adults and children to develop agency and a sense of self-efficacy.

A challenge posed to developing a 'therapeutic alliance' in practice can be the complex trauma that people may have experienced which could mean that they are mistrusting of workers and of services and this can be personally difficult for practitioners. So, in order to overcome this, as well as displaying empathy, warmth and respect, we need to tune in to ourselves and to consider our own feelings about the relationship and supervision is a space to help us to identify any blocks that may be getting in the way of collaborative working.

Developing positive relationships with other professionals to support positive outcomes and using the values highlighted earlier such as empathy and respect need to be adopted, particularly where professional values and purpose may differ. Being aware of other organisational cultures, ethos and priorities can help to build mutually trusting relationships to benefit people who use services.

Examples of theory that underpins this element

- Brief therapies and strengths-based practices such as solution-focused practice (De Shazer *et al.*, 2007; Selekman, 2005; Shennan, 2019)
- Motivational interviewing (Miller and Rollnick, 2013)
- Relational practices (Dix, Hollinrake and Meade, 2019; Megele, 2015; Ruch, Turney and Ward, 2010; Stephenson and Dix, 2025)
- Signs of Safety (Turnell and Edwards (1999)

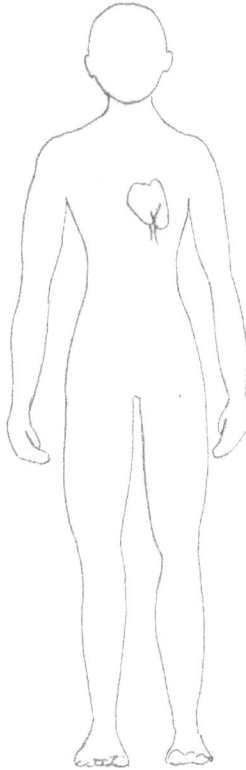

Figure 8.5 The heart as alliance

• Carl Rogers 3 core conditions of empathy, congruence and unconditional positive regard (1961).

This has clear links to influence and the use of legitimate authority included in the Influence aspect of the model and in terms of the metaphor of the body, influences described as the blood supply and so we consider Alliance to be the heart as it is what keeps the blood flowing and enables influence to occur (Figure 8.5).

Support

The above four elements are all focused on the knowledge, skills and values of the practitioner, and in order for these to be present, then organisational Support is required. In order for practitioners to become research-aware and to

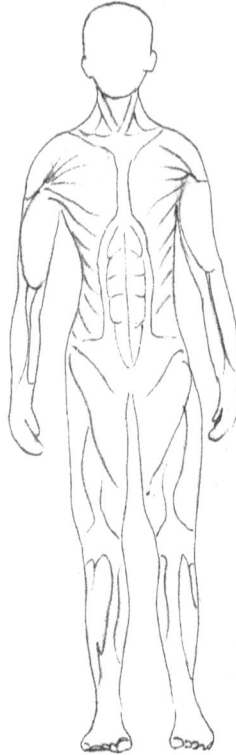

Figure 8.6 The muscles as support

develop critical thinking skills, managers need to be able to facilitate learning and organisational support throughout the layers of the organisation. This includes quality Continuous Professional Development (CPD) opportunities, as well as critically reflective supervision and supportive team cultures that foster a culture of learning as where practitioners can be supported to build on what they are doing well and to link this to research and evidence. Supporting wellbeing is a key aspect of developing professional expertise by ensuring that resilience, emotional intelligence, use of self, sound decision making and reflective thinking skills underpin the effective use and application of the other parts of the model.

So, we consider this aspect of the model to be the muscles that hold everything together, and the more they are used, the better the body can function and the stronger it becomes (Figure 8.6).

So really there is nothing new here in Table 8.1, but **IDEAS** pulls together the thinking and evidence available into an accessible and comprehensive way to form

Table 8.1 Summary of the IDEAS framework

Influence	• Positive use of the professional role to effective change
	• Awareness of structural barriers and inequalities and commitment to anti-discriminatory, anti-oppressive and anti-racist practice
	'The blood supply'
Delivery	• Understanding the professional role and boundaries and limitations
	• Working with statutory frameworks and policy and practice guidance
	• Using the professional tools and systems that support practice and the ability to use these with skill
	• Balancing this element with other parts of the model for it to achieve positive outcomes for people
	'The skeleton'
Expertise	• An understanding of the existing evidence base in a specific field of practice and being able to apply this skilfully
	• Engaging in reflective and reflexive practice
	• Creative and innovative practice
	'The mind'

(Continued)

Table 8.1 *(Continued)*

Alliance	• A commitment to participatory and co-produced ways of working • Knowledge of self *'The heart'*
Support	• The provision of continued professional development opportunities • Effective, critically reflective supervision • A culture of learning at all levels of the organisation *'The muscles'*

a mapping tool to enable individuals and organisations to review their practice. The model also helps to reconcile different ends of the spectrum that are often believed to be in conflict, such as relationship-based practice on one side and research-informed practice on the other.

Application to practice

The following are ways in which the **IDEAS** framework has been applied in practice, although I suspect there are many other ways, so use your inner creativity!

- Practitioners can use the model as part of individual reflection, or through more formal supervision. Each aspect of the model can be mapped out each to help practitioners to think where their strengths are, where they are most confidence and also to identify and training or development needs they have.

- Practitioners can also use it when they are preparing to move to a new role, or position and even as part of the preparation for the interview process to determine what they need to know.
- Students and apprentices have told me that they have used the model when they are starting a placement or rotation as it has helped them to consider what they need to research which has helped them to be more confident.
- It can be used by practice educators to effectively teach, supervise and assess students. It can also be a helpful tool for off-site practice educators who may not have practice knowledge of a specialism to help them to think about what they need to know as a minimum to work with the student.
- It can be used as a quality assurance tool by leaders to develop a culture of effective, relational practice within organisations as it outlines the skills, knowledge and personal attitudes that evidence suggests are necessary to be an effective practitioner and could underpin the principles of the organisation or service and be reflected in the quality assurance tool that is used.
- See below for the use of the **IDEAS** framework to support anti-racist practice and defensible decision making.

TOOL 2: THE IDEAS APPROACH TO ANTI-RACIST PRACTICE

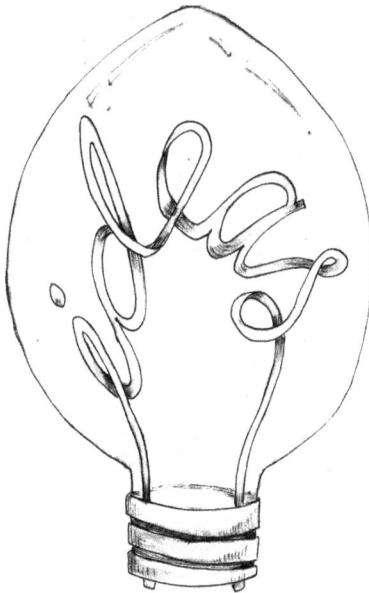

Figure 8.7 Tool 2: The IDEAS approach to anti-racist practice

Introduction

As well as a tool to support quality assurance and reflective, relational practice, the **IDEAS** framework (Figure 8.7) can also help practitioners to be anti-racist in their practice to support safety and wellbeing. Dabiri (2021) suggests that white people need to move beyond ideas of ally-ship which she says is of limited use as it is often performative and does not involve any direct action to challenge for change. Instead, she suggests that white people could seek to make connections through understanding ways they may encounter their own discrimination and oppression (albeit not racism) through, for example, experience sexism, ableism and heteronormality which can lead to social action.

Inspiration

Social work has a long history of activism and anti-racist practices, and this commitment has been strengthened in recent years by the murder of George Floyd in 2020. During this time, I was teaching Black perspectives and white privilege on a university social work programme and white students would often say to me they were committed to being anti-racist in their practice and would find it helpful to consider what this looks like in practice and have a model or framework to guide them. Inspired by Thompson's PCS model (2021) and Tedam's 4D2P framework (2021), I started to consider how **IDEAS** *could support students and practitioners to be anti-racist in their practice.*

Table 8.2 below presents *how* IDEAS can support anti-racist practice:

Example of using ideas to support anti-racist practice

Ella is a white, British woman in her 30s working with Tyreece, a 15-year-old child whose heritage is white British and Black (Jamaican) British. At court Tyreece recently received a 12-month Youth Rehabilitation Order for Robbery. As part of his work with Ella, Tyreece told her that he is being stopped and searched by the police all the time, and when he is with his white friends, it is only him who is being stopped and he is often not told why the search is taking place. Ella is aware that Black males are more likely to be stopped and searched than their white counterparts and found that this was true in local statistics for the area in which Tyreece lives (Expertise). Ella did some work with Tyreece as part of his youth justice plan, so he was aware of his rights in relation to the stop and search process (Delivery and Expertise). She also found a local charity that advocates for racial equality who runs a youth work project

Table 8.2 How IDEAS could support students and practitioners to be anti-racist in their practice

Influence	**What?**
	Use the authority in your role to challenge the following issues encountered in practice when working with risk and uncertainty:
	• discrimination
	• oppression
	• racism
	• micro-aggressions
	• misuse of power and privilege
	How?
	This may include advocating for people when racism is present by respectfully questioning and 'elegantly' challenging colleagues and professionals from other disciplines to promote change. Confronting people head on rarely changes people's thoughts and behaviours as when pushed into a corner we are more likely to become defensive and hold our position. Instead focus on the change you wish to achieve, think about the best time and place to do this and use positive language.
Delivery	**What?**
	Consider the impact of structural inequalities, racism and the resulting trauma in risk assessments.
	How?
	If you are struggling to engage with a person, consider if this is due to who you represent and a lack of mistrust in services and communicate openly and honestly to overcome this.
	Make plans that address any inequalities that exist, e.g. feeling safe in the local community, access to services such as transport, health, housing, education, training, employment.
Expertise	**What?**
	Understand how racism impacts your area of practice and the long-term effects of this on safety and wellbeing. For example, if you are working with children, we know that research indicates that at school Black and mixed ethnic boys are more likely than white boys to be permanently excluded from school (Timpson Review 2019).
	How?
	Seek out your organisation's statement and commitment to anti-racism and any plans they have in place to address this.
	Become familiar with your organisational policies, practice guidance and standards that address exclusions for Black children. If these do not exist, question this with your manager/staff network/equality impact assessment panel.

(Continued)

Table 8.2 *(Continued)*

Alliance	**What?**
	Moving beyond 'allyship' to 'solidarity'.
	How?
	Consider the power and privilege you hold and use these positively to elegantly challenge racism and racist practices in line with social work values. BASW's Code of Ethics suggests that social workers should use the legitimate authority in their role 'in a responsible, accountable and respectful manner' (2021).
	Ask questions and talk with people about their experiences of racism and be ready to listen to what they have to say. Be inquisitive about people's identities and explore this with them. Acknowledge and show empathy for people's experiences.
	Make connections and work collaboratively with community groups to address local issues to challenge for change.
Support	**What?**
	The organisation needs to have structures in place to ensure that anti-racism is embedded throughout the culture of the organisation.
	How?
	Organisational plans and strategies exist to address under- or over-representation of racialised groups in services.
	The provision of specific anti-racist training (as opposed to unconscious bias training).
	Support groups and networks for staff from global majorities.
	There are tools available to enable managers to provide anti-racist supervision that can help to challenge individual and organisational assumptions and biases such as the template created by members of BASW's Black and Ethnic Minority Professionals Symposium (BPS), see their website for more details:
	https://basw.co.uk/about-social-work/psw-magazine/articles/anti-racism-supervision-template-eradicate-colour-blind.

and linked Tyreece into this, picking him up and taking him to the first few sessions (Alliance). *Ella also spoke to her manager about Tyreece's experiences and her manager escalated this to the Head of Service who said that she would speak with police colleagues* (use of Influence and Support from the organisation).

How to use the tool

Consider the different aspects of **IDEAS** outlined above and use the checklist when completing assessments, devising plans and working collaboratively with people who use services together with their personal and professional networks. The **IDEAS approach to anti-racist practice** can also be used by practice managers in group or individual supervision, or as a tool to support peer reflection and by practice educators in their work with students and apprentices.

TOOL 3: THE IDEAS APPROACH TO SUPPORT DEFENSIBLE DECISION MAKING

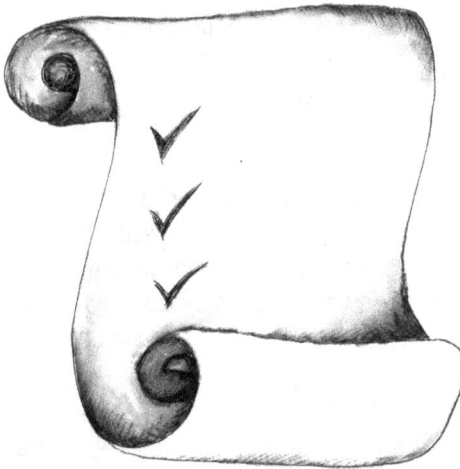

Figure 8.8 Tool 3: The IDEAS approach to support defensible decision making

Introduction

It is often argued that modern social work is becoming more complex due to changes in society such as the evolution of the internet and on-line spaces, as well as the impact of government policies such as austerity which means that people are often in crisis before they meet statutory thresholds for services. Being transparent and accountable for our actions are necessary to inspire trust and confidence to build effective relationships with users of services, as well as colleagues from other professions such as health and the police. Balancing individual rights and freedoms with duties and responsibilities to protect people from harm is a constant balancing act, and social workers can often feel vulnerable and fearful of making mistakes as explored in Chapter 3. When making decisions, adhering to the principles of **defensible decision making** based on the work of Hazel Kemshall (1997a) can help balance rights with duties to protect the safety and wellbeing of everyone.

Inspiration

Many years ago, I attended conference themed around working effectively with risk in youth justice. The keynote speaker spoke about practitioners often experiencing sleepless nights due to the challenges of working with uncertainty. The speaker's comments resonated with my personal experiences of feeling anxious at times about the decisions that I was making. This led me to think about how I could use the **IDEAS framework alongside the features of defensible decision making** *to create a checklist to support practitioners and managers in their work to identify and manage risk to enable us to sleep more soundly at night.*

How to use the tool

The tool (Table 8.3) can be used as a checklist for individual practitioners to consider and record their practice (Figure 8.8), or it can be used collaboratively by managers and practitioners in supervision to explore the rationale behind decisions that have been made. It can also be used by practice educators with students as a learning and teaching aid to help them to think through and evaluate their practice.

Using the checklist can help to avoid defensive practices (sometimes referred to as 'covering your back') and instead assists positive risk management. We are unable to predict the future with certainty and do not have the benefit of hindsight, so there may be times when the decisions we make do not support positive outcomes. However, using this checklist ensures that our decision making is transparent and accountable.

Key points

1   Working with risk and uncertainty requires practitioners to draw on IDEAS to work relationally with users of services and other professionals to promote safety and wellbeing.
2   Being anti-racist involves action and 'challenging for change'.
3   Risk cannot be eliminated and so using the principles of defensible decision making can help practitioners and managers to be transparent and confident in their work to identify and manage risk.

Table 8.3 Using the IDEAS framework alongside the features of defensible decision making

IDEAS	Defensible Decision Making	Actions
Influence and Delivery	Information	• Ensure that information has been collected from a range of sources, including from the child/adult and their personal and professional network. • Triangulate this information with other evidence you have gathered. • Evaluate the information you are using and consider how reliable this is, e.g. are there any gaps, or missing information required to make an effective decision? • Consider the reliability of the sources that you have used.
Expertise and Alliance	Analysis	• Thoroughly analyse the information collated. • Balance risk and protective factors. • Consider different hypotheses and alternative views. • Weigh up different outcomes and options before making a decision. • Check for assumptions, stereotypes and biases on both individual and organisational levels. For example, are policies and procedures inclusive?
Delivery and Expertise	Evidence	• Ensure that decisions made are informed by the latest research evidence and based on the information available at the time. • A clear link can be seen between the information, gathered, the analysis/hypothesis made and any actions that follow.

(Continued)

Table 8.3 *(Continued)*

IDEAS	Defensible Decision Making	Actions
Delivery and Support	Procedures	• Decisions and actions that follow are in line with statutory and legislative responsibilities/duties. • Organisational policies and procedures have been followed. • Have you taken reasonable steps that would be expected?
Delivery and Alliance	Planning	• Risk has been effectively identified using all the information and evidence available. • Risk management plans match the identified risk and are appropriately resourced.
Influence, Delivery, Expertise, Alliance and Support	Communication	• Information and decisions have been shared with members of the personal and professional network. • Be open to respectful questioning and challenge about decisions made linked to supporting information and evidence. • Use supervision to evaluate and review decisions.
Delivery	Recorded	• Record the rationale for the decision made and who has been involved and informed. • Note any differences of views or opinions and evidence why a different decision or course of action was taken.

REFERENCES

Bandura, A. (1971) *Social learning theory*. New York: General Learning Press.

Bell, L.A. (2007) 'Theoretical foundations for social justice education', in Adams, M., Bell, L. A. and Griffin, P. (eds.) *Teaching for diversity and social justice*. 2nd edn. New York: Routledge/Taylor & Francis Group, pp. 1–14.

British Association of Social Workers (BASW) (2018) 80–20 Campaign. *How much 'direct' time do social workers spend with children and families?* Available at: https://basw.co.uk/sites/default/files/2023-08/FINAL%2080-20%20report.pdf Accessed 26/01/25.

British Association of Social Workers (BASW) (2021) *Code of Ethics*. Available at: https://basw.co.uk/policy-practice/standards/code-ethics#guidance Accessed 23/02/25.

Care Act (2014) c. 23. Available at: https://www.legislation.gov.uk/ukpga/2014/23/contents Accessed 26/01/25.

Dabiri, E. (2021) *What white people can do next. from ally-ship to coalition*. Dublin: Penguin/Random House.

De Shazer, S., Dolan, Y., with Korman, H., Trepper, T., McCollum, E. and Kim Berg, I. (2007) *More than miracles: The state of the art of solution-focused brief therapy*. Oxon: Routledge.

Dix, H., Hollinrake, S. and Meade, J. (2019) *Relationship-based practice with adults*. St Albans: Critical Publishing.

French, J.R.P. Jr. and Raven, B. (1959). 'The bases of social power', in Cartwright, D. (ed.) *Studies in social power*. Michigan: University of Michigan, pp. 150–167.

Howe, D. (1998) 'Relationship-based thinking and practice in social work', *Journal of Social Work Practice*, 16(2), pp. 45–56.

Kemshall, H. (1997a) *The management and assessment of risk: Training pack*. London: Home Office.

Megele, C. (2015) *Psychosocial and relationship-based practice*. Northwich: Critical Publishing.

Miller, W. and Rollnick, S. (2013*). Motivational interviewing helping people change.* 3rd edn. New York: Guildford Press.

Munro, E. (2011) *The Munro review of child protection: Final report. A child-centred system*. London: The Stationary Office.

Rappaport, J. (1981) 'In praise of paradox: A social policy of empowerment over prevention', *American Journal of Community Psychology*, 9(1), pp. 1–25.

Rex, S. and Maltravers, A. (1998) *Pro-social modelling and legitimacy*. Cambridge: University of Cambridge Institute of Criminology.

Rogers, C. (1961) *On becoming a person: A therapists view of psychotherapy*. London: Constable.

Ruch, G. (2009) 'Identifying 'the critical' in a relationship-based model of reflection', *European Journal of Social Work*, 12(3), pp. 349–362.

Ruch, G., Turney, D. and Ward, A. (2010) *Relationship-based social work getting to the heart of practice*. London: Jessica Kingsley.

Selekman, M.D. (2005) *Pathways to change brief therapy with difficult adolescents*. 2nd edn. New York: Guilford Press.

Shennan, G. (2019) *Solution-focused practice effective communication to facilitate change*. 2nd edn. London: Red Globe Press.

Stephenson, M. and Dix, H. (2025) *Relational practice in youth justice*. Norwich: Unitas.

Taylor, B. and Devine, T. (1993) *Assessing needs and planning care in social work*. Hants, Aldershot: Arena Ashgate Publishing Limited.

Tedam, P. (2021) *Anti-oppressive social work practice*. London: Learning Matters/Sage.

Thompson, N. (2021) *Anti-discriminatory practice*. 7th edn. London: Red Globe Press.

Timpson, E. (2019) Review of school exclusions available at: https://assets.publishing.service.gov.uk/media/5cfe7d8de5274a0906be72c8/Timpson_review.pdf. Accessed 23/02/25.

Trevithick, P. (2014) 'Humanising managerialism: Reclaiming emotional reasoning, intuition, the relationship, and knowledge and skills in social work', *Journal of Social Work*, 28(3), pp. 287–311.

Turnell, A. and Edwards, S. (1999) *Signs of safety: A safety and solution orientated approach to child protection casework*. New York: W.W. Norton & Company Inc.

Chapter 9
Summary

Heidi Dix and Aisha Howells

Figure 9.1 Summary

Social work is a field which operates within the most complex human issues and a sphere fraught with risk. As a multi-faceted concept, it is argued that risk has replaced all other aspects of the profession's primary mission, such as welfare (Stalker, 2003), making risk a fundamental part of day-to-day practice. However, there is a current culture of fear and risk aversion which practitioners are operating within, alongside expectations to take actions to reduce risk and minimise harm. In some instances, this has meant that Social Workers can tend to practise defensively, rather than the critical, reflexive and careful judgements of 'defensible decisions'. But risk cannot be entirely eradicated, and instead of avoiding risk, practitioners are uniquely trained to

DOI: 10.4324/9781041054740-10

tackle uncertainty head-on and these are areas they can clearly excel in. Risk and uncertainty are the norm, whether that's working in ambiguous situations involving assessment and people with lived experience, navigating systems effectively, or even critical reflexive thinking in order to develop insight about themselves and their relational practice. From safeguarding in child protection, interrogating cycles of trauma and mental health with adults or identifying risks of harm with children involved in youth justice, risk is a powerful influence in social work practice which carries profound, life-changing implications for the individual as well as Social Workers, themselves. Consequently, practitioners' abilities to understand and manage uncertainty are indicative of their duties and responsibilities in gathering information to effectively make decisions. Often, there is a careful balancing act at play where the stakes are high, which forms a key part of sound, ethical, evidence-informed social work practice (Figure 9.1).

Creativity is central to managing and addressing risk, yet is often undervalued in social work. It is rooted within the fabric of what practitioners do – from problem-solving, thinking outside the box, being adaptable and resourceful and unearthing what really might be going on within a situation, beyond surface-level understanding. Conventional approaches may not always be the most appropriate way to navigate risk and this book shows how creative and innovative tools of practice can foster diverse outcomes and propel different ways of thinking. In the introduction, we spoke about how ideas of risk are often based on binary concepts and framed how traditional approaches to risk management tend to focus on the following six key principles:

1   Clear about who is at risk
2   Identification of the risk (what it is)
3   How likely it is to happen (imminence)
4   When it can happen (context)
5   What the impact will be (severity)
6   What will increase and decrease the risk

The tools in this book are the catalyst for practitioners to embrace fresh perspectives, spark new ideas and challenge themselves to step into uncertainty. Together, they are centred towards addressing the above six key principles through creatively different angles. Creativity is inherently connected to change and a reimagination of approaches, evolving beyond the limits of established, standardised practices and static conditions. As such, these tools present synergy between practice, risk and innovation and, consequently, cultivate meaningful creativity to thrive in social work.

Figure 9.2 Heidi and Aisha

Artwork Heidi and Aisha Illustration by Ava Howells

We hope this book fills your social work practice with courage, beauty and inspiration!

Heidi and Aisha (Figure 9.2)

REFERENCE

Stalker, K. (2003) 'Managing risk and uncertainty in social work: A literature review', *Journal of Social Work: JSW*, 3(2), pp. 211–233.

Index

Note: Page references with *Italics* refer to figures, **bold** refer to tables.

For Product Safety Concerns and Information please contact our EU
representative GPSR@taylorandfrancis.com
Taylor & Francis Verlag GmbH, Kaufingerstraße 24, 80331 München, Germany

www.ingramcontent.com/pod-product-compliance
Lightning Source LLC
Chambersburg PA
CBHW052007270326
41929CB00015B/2816

9 781916 925960